SOME EXPERIENCES

OF

A BARRISTER'S LIFE

BY

MR SERJEANT BALLANTINE

IN TWO VOLUMES

VOL. I.

THIRD EDITION

LONDON

RICHARD BENTLEY & SON, NEW BURLINGTON STREET

Publishers in Ordinary to Her Majesty the Queen

1882

Printing Statement:

Due to the very old age and scarcity of this book,
many of the pages may be hard to read due to the
blurring of the original text, possible missing pages,
missing text and other issues beyond our control.

Because this is such an important and rare work, we
believe it is best to reproduce this book regardless of
its original condition.

Thank you for your understanding.

PREFATORY NOTE.

I HAVE FELT AT A LOSS to know in what manner
I ought to introduce the following pages to the
reader, and should have been inclined to launch
them without a word of preface, but that it might
be thought that I formed an exaggerated estimate
of their intrinsic worth, which certainly is not the
case.

What I have striven to do, and trust I have
succeeded in doing, has been to adhere strictly to
facts in the incidents related; and the conclusions
expressed are the honest results of such experience
as a long professional life, not unmixed with other
associations, has enabled me to form.

If my lighter sketches should amuse a leisure
hour, my object will have been attained; and if
any suggestions upon graver topics should furnish

hints leading to any more useful end, I shall be amply rewarded.

It may be permitted to me to add, that whilst writing in no presumptuous spirit, I have not hesitated, upon some subjects, to express my opinions with perfect frankness and candour.

Wm. BALLANTINE.

The Temple:
March 1882.

NOTE TO THE THIRD EDITION.

I MAY be permitted to say a few words by way of apology for some errors that have been very kindly pointed out to me. I fear that they have generally arisen from my trusting too implicitly to my memory. The edition now appearing has progressed too far to enable me to correct the whole of them, but there is one that I wish at once to set right, namely, my statement that Baron Bolland was the only judge appointed by Lord Lyndhurst (vol. i. p. 148).

At a future time I will explain the origin of the blunder.

Wm. BALLANTINE.

Union Club: *April* 13, 1882.

CONTENTS

OF

THE FIRST VOLUME.

———◦◦———

CHAPTER I.

AUTOBIOGRAPHY.

CHAPTER II.

LONDON DURING MY PUPILAGE.

CHAPTER III.

COMMENCEMENT OF MY PROFESSIONAL LIFE.

CHAPTER IV.

MY EARLY PERFORMANCES.

CHAPTER V.

CHOICE OF CIRCUIT.

CHAPTER VI.

THE THAMES POLICE COURT.

CHAPTER VII.

THE TRIAL OF COURVOISIER.

CHAPTER XI.

FAMOUS AUTHORS.

CHAPTER XII.

LORD LYNDHURST.

CHAPTER XIII.

MR. BARON PARKE.

CHAPTER XIV.

IMPRESSIONS OF SWITZERLAND AND HOMBURG.

CHAPTER XV.

LORD CAMPBELL.

CHAPTER XVI.

CAMPBELL'S IRRITABILITY.

CHAPTER XVII.

I BECOME A SERJEANT.

CHAPTER XVIII.

THE GARRICK CLUB.

CHAPTER XIX.

INEQUALITY OF SENTENCES.

SOME EXPERIENCES

OF

A BARRISTER'S LIFE.

———◆———

CHAPTER I.

AUTOBIOGRAPHY.

HOWLAND STREET, Tottenham Court Road, was, as
I have heard, the place of my birth. My first
memories, however, are of a farmhouse—I have
none of how I got there. I remember a large
yard, and plenty of straw to roll about in; the
pigs and the poultry were my earliest friends,
freedom and fresh air my happiness. It was at
Warboys, a small village in Huntingdonshire.
The property belonged to my mother, who was a
native of Somersham of the same county.

These happy days were terminated by a long
journey. Stuffed inside a coach, I was sick and
miserable, and was scolded for being troublesome.
I remember perfectly being deposited in a dull

dreary home, which I now know was No. 1 Serjeants' Inn, Fleet Street, and have a distinct impression how sour the bread tasted. It is strange
that so trivial a circumstance should remain upon
the memory when many much more important are
obliterated, and it is only on that account that I
have thought it worth recording.

From this period my mind is a blank, until
I was sent to a school at Fulham, kept by two
maiden ladies of the name of Batsford. I have no
recollection of what I learnt, or how I was taught;
but the Sundays passed there have remained graven
on my mind—Marched, two and two, to the parish
church, clad in our best clothes, and encased in a sort
of moral strait-waistcoat; cramped up in a narrow
pew, prayer-book in hand, listening to what we could
not understand, we strove, often ineffectually, to
keep awake, knowing that if we yielded to drowsi-
ness we forfeited our share of the pudding—sole
pleasure of the day.

Oh ! how I envied the swallows, as they flitted
across the windows in joyous sport, revelling in
the blessings given them by God, and forbidden to
us upon the Sunday. I do not remember how long I
remained under the charge of these ladies, of whom
I still retain kindly recollections.

My father had originally been in the army, but
at the period of my birth had been called to the

bar. He carried on his profession, as well as lived, in Serjeants' Inn, Fleet Street. My mother, at the time of her marriage, was a young lady of wealth and position in Huntingdonshire. The house in which we dwelt was the reverse of lively, and I fancy that my father's fortunes were not at that time prosperous. My mother was a most excellent and pious woman, and carried out with conscientious rigour the views of Sunday which had prevailed at our school. I was taken regularly to the Temple Church, and never will the memory of the hours passed within those solemn walls be effaced from my mind. Under the influence of the Rev. Mr. Rowlett, a most worthy but not enlivening clergyman, I too frequently yielded to the sleepy god, and for doing so received present punishment and was promised a terrific future. A worthy old nurse, of the Baptist persuasion, who would not willingly have hurt a fly, helped to fill my soul with terrors; and at the top of our dreary house, in a lonely bedroom, the memory of my offences and the anticipation of their penalty drove me nearly frantic.

Unheard and unpitied, I many a time cried myself to sleep. The relation also of any horrible crime used to produce a most painful effect upon me in my lonely moments, and I particularly remember hearing talked about the murder of a Mrs. Donathy, an old lady living in James

Street, Bedford Row. It caused a great sensation at the time, and it is wonderful, after a long lapse of years, how vivid my recollection of it is. The thought of it was present to me at night, and every noise conjured up a murderer to my imagination. Such memories remain—perhaps, also, their consequences.

The Temple Gardens relieved the monotony of our domicile, but even there I felt that the lynx eyes of the gardener were watching my every movement.

I cannot say what period of my life was thus occupied, but I remember one magical and delightful event. I was taken to see a pantomime. How wonderful it was, and how beautiful! I have never forgotten it. I even now remember a scene in which, in a snowstorm, Baron Munchausen fastened his horse to the steeple of a church, mistaking it for a gate, and the next morning, the snow having melted, there was the steed dancing upon air. Great was my ecstasy when the Baron, taking aim with his gun, separated the reins from the steeple, and the horse came tumbling down. And there was another welcome treat in my existence, when I went on a brief visit to one of my father's sisters. She lived at Wimbledon, and was married to the Rev. Joshua Ruddock, who prepared a few lads for the University. With what pleasure I recall their loving hospitality, the delight of roving on the Common and over the Danish Camp, the little present of books long looked forward to, which terminated my happy sojourn.

Once my brother and myself were taken to the seaside—Broadstairs, afterwards a favourite resort of Charles Dickens. The mode by which this pleasant watering-place was then reached was by two steam-packets. I remember their names—the ' Engineer ' and ' Majestic.' They had nearly superseded the old Margate hoys, which, however, like the stage-coaches with the railways in a future generation, were then maintaining a hopeless contest with their formidable rivals. I believe that. these were the first steamers upon the Thames,[1] and were allowed to die a natural death at a. mature age, after a prosperous career. Their successors, although not extinct, have to a great extent yielded to the convenience and speed of conveyance by rail, and now, of the many thousands who in the course of a year visit the Isle of Thanet, only a small proportion select this very agreeable mode of reaching it.

On the morning following our arrival at Broadstairs, which had not been until late on the preceding evening, for the first time the broad

---

[1] They were certainly the first that ran to Margate.

expanse of the ocean disclosed itself to my aston-
ished senses.   I can but inadequately describe the
sensation it occasioned.   It must have been calm,
with a summer haze brooding lazily over its surface,
whilst to my unaccustomed eyes distant vessels
seemed suspended from the sky.   Once only, since
that time, have I experienced the same feeling
of wonderment and awe, and that was when, many
years after, the view of a long range of snowy
mountains burst upon my vision.   On such occasions as these something seems added to our nature,
exalting and purifying it.   The sands, too, were a
source of intense enjoyment.   But most of my
readers have had this illustrated by means more
vivid than words, in the happy faces of the urchins
playing upon the beach.   Many pleasant hours
have I since passed in the same locality : but what
can ever replace the joyousness that knows no
remorse for the past or fear for the future !

A contrast came only too soon : the blackest
and most odious period of my existence arrived—I
was sent to St. Paul's School.   The house was then
standing where it does now in the churchyard ; but,
shortly after I entered, the school was removed to
Aldersgate Street whilst the present building was
being erected.

I was a day scholar.[1]   There were four masters,

---

[1] Some boys boarded with the masters.

all clergymen. Dr. Sleath was at the head. Of
him I knew nothing except by sight, never having
reached the classes over which he presided. He
was a man of portly presence, a good scholar, I
believe, and much respected. Bean, Edwards, and
Durham were the three other instructors, and,
however different these were in many respects,
they possessed one common attribute. They were
all tyrants—cruel, cold-blooded, unsympathetic
tyrants. Armed with a cane, and surrounded by
a halo of terror, they sat at their respective
desks. Under Durham the smaller boys trembled ;
Edwards took the next in age. Each flogged con-
tinuously. The former, a somewhat obese personage, with a face as if cut out of a suet-pudding, was
solemn in the performance of this, his favourite
occupation. . The Rev. Mr. Edwards, on the contrary, though a cadaverous-looking object, was quite
funny over the tortures he inflicted. Trois Echelles
and Petit André, the executioners of Louis XI., so
admirably described by Walter Scott in his novel
of ' Quentin Durward,' treated their victims after
a similar fashion. One of the favourite modes
of inflicting pain adopted by these tyrants was,
when the boys came in on a winter's morning,
shivering and gloveless, to strike them violently
with the cane over the tips of their fingers. I
nearly learnt at that school the passion of hatred,

and should probably have done so but that my mind was too fully occupied by terror. Bean was a short, podgy, pompous man, with insignificant features. His mode of correction was different in form, and I can see him now, with flushed, angry face, lashing some little culprit over back and shoulders until his own arm gave way under the exertion. Amongst the amusements of this gentleman, one was to throw a book—generally Entick's Dictionary, if I remember rightly—at the head of any boy who indulged in a yawn, and, if he succeeded in his aim and produced a reasonable contusion, he was in good humour for the rest of the day. I have met them all three since my school days, and found them shallow and ignorant, no doubt with plenty of Greek and Latin in their heads, but without knowledge of human nature or power of appreciating the different dispositions of their pupils. All that was necessary for them to know was that they were capable of suffering. I have heard that of late years the school has been admirably conducted, and has turned out brilliant scholars ; but I am not aware that any of my contemporaries obtained in their subsequent careers great distinction. There were, of course, the ordinary catalogue of minor nuisances in the shape of very good boys and very great bullies.

I was always badly dressed, and seldom had

any money in my pocket. This was no fault of my poor mother, and I fancy, as I have before hinted, that at that time the *res angusta* pervaded our household. It is a bad thing for a boy to be sent to a school in a worse plight than his fellow-pupils; it is apt to breed meanness in himself, and invariably subjects him to tyranny from others. Of the latter I underwent my full share. I suspect I was a bit of a coward; I know I hated fighting. There was a fat brute named Thomson who used to thrash me unmercifully, but one afternoon I hurt his head with a leaden inkstand, and, although I got well caned for this little accident, I found it had a good effect on my persecutors.

I may mention that during the time I was attending this school my father had removed from No. 1 to No. 6 in the same Inn, and that amongst its other inhabitants were Serjeant Wilde, afterwards Lord Truro, Frederick Pollock, afterwards Chief Baron, and Mr. Jervis, a Welsh judge, father of the future Chief Justice of the Common Pleas.

On my way to school I had to pass an ancient inn, called the 'Bolt in Tun.' It was situated on the south side of Fleet Street. Its sign as well as name breathed memories of the past—The Arrow into the Target. There was generally a four-horse coach standing opposite its gateway. How I lingered, gazing with admiring eyes at coachman and horses! How I envied the passengers! They were about to quit smoky London and breathe the fresh air of the fields. They had no dread of the cane descending upon frozen fingers. I knew what would be my fate; but still I looked and longed, and turned to take one look more. I could not picture unhappiness in the hearts of the passengers. I ran on to my gloomy lot, hoping not to be late; but if I were, that I should get some warmth into my trembling hands.

After I had been at St. Paul's some four or five years, my father took a house at Hampstead, and, to my great joy, I was sent to a school at Blackheath, called Ashburnham House, kept by Mr. Wigan. This gentleman was a scholar, and both kind and considerate to his pupils. He had a brother a physician in Finsbury Square,[1] and his sons Alfred and Horace, subsequently distinguished actors, were amongst my fellow-pupils. The school was not financially a success, and broke up. I went afterwards to another private school at Hampstead, kept by worthy people named Johnson, and in the air of this most pleasant of suburban places I soon regained my spirits and

---

[1] I have mentioned this connection of Mr. Wigan in consequence of an utterly false account that I saw in a recent publication of the position of Mr. Alfred Wigan's parents.

looked more contentedly upon life. Here I remained for some years, having little to record until I commenced the graver studies of the law.

And I now propose to sketch, very briefly, my career up to the time when I obtained permission from the Honourable Society of the Inner Temple to gain what livelihood I could in the position of a barrister.

At the period when I was looking forward to this event, there might be seen in different parts of London an individual of somewhat eccentric appearance. He was a thin active old gentleman with powdered hair, and I believe a pigtail— certainly with knee-breeches and silk stockings. This was Mr. Platt, clerk to the celebrated Lord Chief Justice, Lord Ellenborough, and father of Thomas Platt, barrister-at-law, Queen's Counsel, and ultimately a baron of the Exchequer. This latter gentleman was a friend of my father, and kindly received me into his chambers, where I remained for some three months. He is worthy of a place in any legal records. Well educated, but with no commanding talent, with no pretence to eloquence, and starting from a comparatively humble position, by industry and perseverance and most upright and honourable conduct, he achieved the high position I have mentioned, with the respect of the public and the profession.

And yet, strange to say, he violated the obvious intentions of nature, and like Liston, the comedian, who imagined himself to have been intended for tragedy, although essentially comic in the form and expression of his features, the subject of my sketch, with a face that seemed made to create laughter, would plant upon it the most lugubrious of looks. ' Pray,' said Lord Lyndhurst to him one day, ' spare us that wife and twelve children face.' Nevertheless, his appeals to common juries were very effective. The following climax, which I remember, greatly increased the damages awarded to a young lady for whom he was counsel : ' And, gentlemen, this serpent in human shape stole the virgin heart of my unfortunate client whilst she was returning from confirmation !'

The Honourable Charles Ewan Law, son of Lord Ellenborough, commenced a career at the bar about the same period as Mr. Platt, and went the same circuit, the Home, with every accompaniment to success except his own demeanour. He undoubtedly possessed ability, but it was smothered by pomposity and vulgar pride.

He signally failed at the bar, but his rank and connection obtained for him the office of Recorder of London, and he was thoroughly ashamed of the patrons who had placed him there. Although I do not consider that there is any merit in being too humane, I still think it fair to say that in his administration of justice he was considerate and merciful. He was in Parliament, but never distinguished himself. I remember, after Mr. Platt became a judge, his presiding at the Central Criminal Court, Mr. Law being then in the inferior position of Recorder.

After leaving Mr. Platt's chambers, I went to those of Mr. William Henry Watson, at that time a pleader below the bar, who afterwards became a Baron of the Exchequer. His father was a general officer, and he had himself commenced his career in the army. He was, I believe, a good case lawyer, and had a large business. He received some ten or a dozen pupils, whom he permitted to learn what they could, and, judging by myself, this was very little. He was a gentleman, and a favourite with all of us. I have little to record of the two years I passed in these chambers amongst a mass of papers, copying precedents of pleading which were a disgrace to common sense, and in gossip with my brother students, most of them as idle as myself. They were older than I was, and amongst them was a gentleman with whom I have remained ever since upon terms of intimacy. This was Mr. Joseph Brown. He was a very hard worker, and used to suffer grievously from the want of that quality in the majority of his fellow-pupils. He became a distinguished leader upon the same circuit with myself, and will go down to posterity as the admired author of the longest set of pleadings ever known. At the bar, his arguments have been most exhaustive, and never weakened by any approach to levity. Socially, his knowledge and learning render him a most delightful and improving companion, and every one who knows him respects and likes him.

John Nodes Dickenson, another pupil, was also a hard worker, and, oddly enough, like myself, had been at the school kept by the Misses Batsford. He also joined the Home circuit, and he and I were accustomed to lodge together at Maidstone. He accepted early in his career a Colonial judgeship. His brother, the eminent Queen's Counsel, has recently retired from the equity bar.

Edward Rushton, familiarly called Ned, was a pupil of a different type. Much older than any of us, he had been an active politician, and amused us with tales of election contests. We believed him to be a great orator. Perhaps he was. Cobbett had given him the name of Roaring Rushton. He became afterwards stipendiary magistrate at Liverpool, his native place.

Hamill, another pupil, obtained the post of a police magistrate of the metropolis. I must not forget, too, 'Ben Hyam,' whose real name was Marriott.

His father was a magistrate, before whom a charge
was made by a Turk, an itinerant vendor of rhubarb,
who had been robbed of all his earnings. The case
was clear enough, and the thief ordered to be committed. The Moslem was told he must appear at
the next sessions. He swore by the Prophet that
he could not; upon which the magistrate, legally
enough, ordered him to find bail for his appearance, which of course he was unable to do, and
went to prison in default. The magistrate, *ex debito
justitiæ*, admitted the prisoner to the same privilege, of which he speedily availed himself. The
sessions arrived, and, as might be expected, the
thief did not. Ben Hyam, after the loss of his
earnings and his liberty, was released. What became of him I never heard, but his reflections upon
English justice could hardly have been higher than
those we entertain about an Eastern cadi. Hence
arose the nickname bestowed on my friend Marriott, which he retained to the day of his death,
which occurred early.

I have met with an account of the above incident as having occurred in Russia, but I can vouch
for the accuracy of my statement, and that it occurred in London about the year 1830.

At last the labours that led to the bar and
might lead to the woolsack were over. I had
eaten the requisite number of dinners. A good

appetite and good digestion rendered this not difficult, and there were pleasant young fellows, full of
hope and high spirits engaged in the same occupation with myself.

The batch to be ' turned off' were summoned to
the bench table. We were each presented with a
glass of wine, and a speech was made to us by the
treasurer, giving us good advice and wishing us
prosperity in our forthcoming career; and so we
were launched upon the sea, looking then so calm,
but, alas! too often engulfing pitilessly the brightest
ventures. Upon these occasions unpleasant truths
were sometimes uttered, and on one of them a gentleman named Carden, who had to return thanks
for his fellow-students, concluded by expressing his
regret that none of those who had wished them
success were likely to live to see it.

I propose in my next chapter to give a glimpse
of London as I remember it during my pupilage,
some of the scenes I witnessed, and the impressions
they conveyed.

CHAPTER II.

LONDON DURING MY PUPILAGE.

IN giving a description of the great metropolis previously to my call, I shall confine myself as nearly as possible to the results of my own observation, and the impressions springing from it. Its surface and extent were very different from those which now present themselves to the view: bricks and mortar, marching in all directions, have eaten up many a green field and pleasant lane; and palaces now cover what were unhealthy swamps or the noisome dwellings of the poorest classes.

It is not, however, the changes only that meet the eye which have to be recorded. Science, literature, thought, have made prodigious strides, and many speculations are now openly discussed upon subjects which it would then have been thought impiety even to allude to. Steam, a sleeping giant, has been forced to work, and panting and puffing has brought people together, adding to their pleasures and enlarging their minds; and, wonder of wonders, more wonderful than any tale of magic, electricity has conquered space, and seems now to be pursuing a career to which there is no apparent limit. Some crimes have assumed larger proportions, and the present has been an age of daring and gigantic fraud.

And yet in those days there existed men worthy of any period in a great nation. The battle of Waterloo was fought in the year 1815, and the greatest general since the time of Marlborough was placed by the enthusiastic voice of the nation upon a pedestal from which in that capacity he has never been displaced, although as a statesman he was unpopular, and persecuted by a thoughtless mob. Walter Scott had only recently published one of the most charming of his works, ' Guy Mannering,' which will for all ages delight young and old. Byron and Shelley had startled sober people by their wondrous poetry and reckless opinions. Great lawyers had adorned the bench, and the bold advocacy of Erskine had done much to cement the liberties of the people, whilst crimes of stupendous atrocity were not without their representatives.

The interests of medical science had created a body of men that have passed into oblivion. Like the ghouls of eastern story, they haunted graveyards, and lived upon corpses, violating the tomb, and gaining a living by supplying the dissecting-table

with its ghastly subjects. They were called re-
surrectionists. It occurred to a native of Edinburgh, named Burke, that an easier and more profitable method might be devised to attain the same
end, and he and an accomplice named Hare established a system of assassination ; lads wandering
about the street were little likely to be missed,
there were few to inquire for them. They might be
half-starving, but still their carcases would serve
the purpose of the surgeon's knife ; and they must
not be spoilt by external damage, and so these
fiends, stealthily crawling behind them, pressed a
pitch plaster over their mouths and noses, and
thus suffocated them. They were then conveyed
to the dissecting-rooms and sold to the anatomists,
fetching a good price, as, unlike many stolen from
the grave, the bodies were comely and free from
corruption. There appears to have been strange
carelessness on the part of the recipients ; they
knew that the class they were dealing with was
infamous, and the appearance of the subjects
ought to have created suspicion ; but it is fair to
remember that probably those best able to form
an opinion were not present at the earlier stages
of the transaction. 'To burke' has become a
recognised word in the English language. No
one doubts that the study of anatomy, pursued
through the means of dissection of dead bodies,

is most useful in the interest of mankind. No
one will dispute the labour, thought, and skill
that have been exercised in its practice, or the
enormous benefits that have been attained by it;
and although there may be a sensational feeling
against it, no real evil is inflicted by its exercise;
and the interests both of science and humanity
fully justify its use.

It is now some fifteen years ago that a man of
middle height and proportionately stout, clad in one
of the ordinary white smocks worn by labourers,
guided by a dog and holding in one of his hands a
metal saucer, might be seen slowly perambulating
the streets of London. His sightless eyes, turned
upwards, appealed to the compassion of the passer
by. This man was Hare, the accomplice of Burke,
who had been admitted as a witness against him.
Subsequently to the trial he obtained employment
in another name upon some limeworks. His fellow-
labourers found out who he was, and threw him
into one of the pits, the contents of which caused
him the loss of his sight. There was a woman who
was accustomed to join him at the end of the day,
and apparently accompany him to wherever he
lived.

I have often seen these two meet, but never
noticed a smile on the face of either of them.

The infamy of this crime was not confined to

Scotland. I remember, when a youth, I was taken to the Old Bailey to see two men tried for the murder of an Italian boy by similar means, and with the same object. It was the first time that I made my appearance in that court, and if I remember rightly I had a seat with the Ordinary. The names of these men were Bishop and Williams; they were both convicted and executed.

In recording the above circumstances my mind naturally reverts to a practice which existed then as it does now, and which I believe is viewed by a great portion of the community with feelings of repulsion and horror. I need hardly say that 1 allude to vivisection. It is said that it promotes knowledge which is serviceable to the human race, and those who practise it defend it upon that ground. If this assertion were conclusively proved, which certainly is not the case, I should still protest against its use, and denounce it as a disgrace to a Christian land. The hypothesis upon which it is defended must be that the brain, muscles, and nerves of an animal are analogous to those of a human being, and therefore will, under certain conditions, exhibit similar results. If so, vivisectionists apply to creatures formed like themselves tortures which the ingenuity of science has rendered more terrible than any invented by the savage.

There can be no doubt that some of their victims do possess thought and memory, affection and gratitude, that might shame their persecutors, but whether these qualities are developed in the same way or are dependent upon the same causes must be matter of speculation. How can the vivisectionist know that when he touches some nerve which makes the unhappy creature writhe in unspeakable agony, the same effect would be produced upon the human frame? Some slight difference may create a complete error in the conclusion arrived at, and a human patient may be treated upon an erroneous assumption that his brain is worked upon by the same influences as that of a dog. If, on the other hand, the assumption is that animals are differently formed from ourselves, it is difficult to embrace the idea that their torture can produce beneficial consequences. I believe that speculation of a kind created by vivisection is more likely to lead to blundering than to benefit, and the reports which I have read of the inquiry before a committee of the House of Commons by no means removes the impression; but as I have already said, if it were proved to demonstration that some benefit might be obtained by it, the practice is not the less abominable and unholy. I believe that the true instincts of every pure heart will throb in sympathy with this feeling. As I write, my old collie, friend and companion for the last ten years, is looking at me with his earnest brown eyes, as if thanking me for this humble protest against the torture of dumb life.[1]

Having alluded to the Duke of Wellington, I may here mention that I once met him at dinner. He was then much aged, talked gravely and with great distinctness, ate but little, drank no wine, and left early. He was a member of the Union Club when I joined it, and I have heard a story that he became a member of Crockford's, the famous gambling resort, that he might blackball his sons if they became candidates. Of course I had heard a great deal about him, after the fashion and with the accuracy usually extended to children by their early informants. I remember the touching anecdote of how he and that old Prussian warrior, Blucher, met upon the field of Waterloo and mingled their tears over the bodies of the slain. The well-known and much more probable story is told of the latter that, having been entertained at a city dinner, and thoroughly enjoyed its gorgeous hospitality, he delighted his hosts by his admiration of London, concluding, however, with

---

[1] This dog when a puppy was given to me by Colonel Farquharson of Invercauld, and I could record instances of his sagacity quite equal . to many attributed to reason in a human being.

the startling exclamation, ' What a splendid city it would be to sack ! '

The Duke afterwards gave a dinner at Apsley House to the Tower Hamlets magistrates. I remember that at the time the Duchess was ill, and the fear of her being disturbed prevented the picture gallery from being lighted up. I constantly met the Duke afterwards, and was always very graciously recognised.[1]

Streets at this period after dark blinked with the aid of oil lamps. A machine called a hackney-coach, licensed to carry six people, redolent of damp straw, driven by a still damper coachman, was the principal mode of locomotion. The driver was called a jarvey, a compliment paid to the class in consequence of one of them named Jarvis having been hanged. Omnibuses were unknown.

Those stalwart figures in blue that are now to be seen lounging gracefully by area steps, were still imbedded in the brain of Sir Robert Peel. Officers called Bow Street runners were supposed to catch thieves, with whom in their convivial hours they associated.

Watchmen—Charlies they were named—called the hours of the night, probably lest by some accident they might disturb offenders. When middle-class people went to a play, or to some

[1] *Vide* Appendix.

little distance out of town, they performed the
operation in what was called a glass coach; why
so called I must leave to antiquarian research.
It did not smell so much of straw as the hackney-
coach, and the driver at some period or other may
have washed himself. It was, however, an eminently respectable vehicle, and naturally, therefore, very slow and solemn in its movements, and
its employment was a great event in the family.
There sprang up, however, in my comparatively
early days, a dissipated-looking vehicle called a
cab. It was formed of an open box placed upon
two high wheels. This was for the passenger;
the driver sat upon a board by the side. They
were considered fast—not so much in motion as in
character. However, the necessity for locomotion
does away with prejudice, and I have lived to see
an archbishop in a hansom cab!

The Church was represented in the main
streets of London by figures that exhibited a
strange appearance to my juvenile mind. These
were the bishops. They then wore white wigs,
surmounted by a three-cornered hat called a
shovel, a long silk apron, knee-breeches, and silk
stockings, for which their legs seldom seemed well
suited. I have often felt grateful that Queen's
Counsel in their robes are exposed to the view of
only a limited circle, and the very thought of

walking through a crowded thoroughfare in my
full-bottomed wig throws me into a cold perspira-
tion.   In the narrow places and byways men
soberly dressed in plain, and sometimes thread-
bare, black, then as now, brought consolation to
the hovels of the poor and starving.   These, a
noble, self-denying race, are the working clergy,
and are confined to no denomination.

London did not boast of so many theatres as
it does now, and the drama scarcely presented any
similar features.   Drury Lane and Covent Garden
were then the principal, and, possessing certain
privileges, were called patent theatres.   The performers were described as Her Majesty's servants.
The legitimate drama, the ordinary entertainment, was varied by farces—not · pieces of buf-
foonery, but comedies in two acts; and the
pantomime at Christmas, then really justifying its
name, was one of the institutions of the country.
To those accustomed to the magnificent scenery,
gorgeous decorations, and the semi-operatic, semi-
burlesque displays now called pantomimes, the simplicity of their predecessors would be astonishing.
They were played in dumb show, and a plot
pervaded the whole.   It was simple enough.   In
the beginning a benevolent fairy announced her
intention of protecting certain virtuous lovers,
whilst a demon was bent upon their destruction.

A tyrannical father and objectionable suitor were patronised by the latter. They constantly followed the virtuous pair, who as constantly eluded their grasp, whilst they themselves met with every kind of misfortune, until they became clown and pantaloon; whilst the lovers were sprightly harlequin and columbine, still persecuted by their old enemies, until the good fairy made them happy in domains of bliss. The tricks and tumbling which characterised the performance were witnessed with shouts of laughter by the urchins who then crowded every part of the house, very different indeed from the gravity that now attends the representations. The pantomime was usually preceded by such dramas as 'Jane Shore' or 'George Barnwell,' whether with the idea of contrast or with a view of inculcating moral lessons I cannot say; but inasmuch as the gods never allowed them to be heard, whatever the purpose was, it had no chance of succeeding.

The names of Kemble, Edmund Kean, Miss O'Neil, and many others adorn the theatrical annals of those days. I have seen the two latter, but must have been too young to appreciate them. I have a vivid recollection of Charles Kemble playing the 'Inconstant,' in the comedy of that name, and every word and gesture of the actor, in his scene with the bravos, remain fresh upon

my memory. Miss Foote was the heroine. How
beautiful she was!

I have been frequently in the company of
Charles Kemble; and I remember on one occasion
dining with him at the Garrick Club. He sat immediately under a life-like picture of a scene from a
drama called the 'Merry Monarch,' in which he represented Charles II. Fawcett played Captain Copp,
and one of the most charming of actresses, Maria
Tree, played Mary. How well also I remember Miss
Love, and the ballad of 'Buy a Broom.' However,
fond as I am of the subject, I must not weary my
readers. Those who also like it, and there are many
less amusing and instructive, will find abundant food
in two pleasant volumes lately published by the
veteran author and stage manager, Mr. Stirling,
and a clever and very entertaining pamphlet called
'Church and Stage,' written by Henry Spicer, an
old and valued friend of mine. The English Opera
House stood upon the site of the present Lyceum.
The only memory I have of it is seeing Miss Kelly
play Meg Merrilies in a version of 'Guy Mannering.'
The old Adelphi, however, a small theatre standing
on the same site as the present building, deserves
special mention. The first piece I remember being
played there was 'Tom and Jerry.' A little unknown
man, who had been given some three lines to say,
contrived in doing so to create roars of laughter.

His part was written up, and from that time to his death he was recognised as one of the most comic actors that ever delighted an audience. This was Robert Keeley, and it is no unjust criticism to say that he was fully equalled by his talented wife, who still lives, and, although she has retired from the stage, is as bright and lively as ever.[1] The glories of the Adelphi would fill a volume. What old patron of the drama will ever forget Yates, Jack Reeve, little Wright, Miss Honey, or that most wonderful of stage villains O. Smith? And even out of this phalanx of talent there stood one figure, Mrs. Yates, the most perfect personator of what may be called domestic drama that ever walked the stage. I had the pleasure of knowing her in private life, where, like many other ladies then and now following the same calling, she was as much respected and admired as she was in her professional career. At the Haymarket Buckstone was in his line without a rival. But I must hurry on. There are many about whom I should like to say a loving word, but space forbids. I must not, however,

---

[1] *July* 21, 1881.—I had the pleasure yesterday, at the house of my hospitable friends, Mr. and Mrs. Levy, to meet this lady, and my description of her is by no means overcharged. She told me that she was seventy-five years old. I had a long and most pleasant talk with her. Mrs. Wigan, the widow of my old schoolfellow, the distinguished actor, herself a most accomplished actress, was also present. It was delightful to see these two old ladies seemingly so happy, and receiving much attention from everybody present.

forget the transpontine theatres, the Surrey and Co-
burg, the latter renamed after our gracious Queen.
Terrific combats signalised their boards; outraged
innocence, diabolical oppression, virtue rewarded,
wickedness punished by means utterly impossible
off the stage, drew crowds of admirers, and filled
the small picture-shops with characteristic likenesses.   One Italian opera house existed, but I do
not fancy that it possessed attractions beyond a
limited circle.   Fashion reigned within its walls,
and I confess that even if I could have obtained
admission I should greatly have preferred a
Surrey melodrama.

Whilst steam and electricity have worked
their magic changes, a boon has been conferred
upon suffering humanity by the application of
anæsthetics.

In my early days there were great surgeons.
The names of Astley Cooper and Brodie, and a
crowd of others, adorned and elevated a noble
profession, but they had to pursue their art
inflicting great pain in alleviating disease.   At
present, happily, sense and feeling sleep whilst the
knife performs its marvellous task.

Let me now take a glimpse at the surface of what
I will call old London and its ways.   Although
there were distinguished lawyers and an imposing

array of courts, justice was slow and expensive.
There were no county courts, but here and there
in the metropolis were dotted small debts courts,
not remarkable for dignity or use; they were
called Courts of Request. Debtors were incarcerated, and suffered frequently worse punishments than criminals. The Queen's Bench prison,
with its misery and its shame, is a thing of the
past, and the sad voice of the poor prisoner is no
longer heard from the walls of the Fleet.[1] Police-
courts were called offices, and the magistrates
might be costermongers; Sir Richard Birnie, the
chief magistrate, was, I believe, a saddler. The
streets at night exhibited scenes of disorder and
unchecked profligacy. The south end of Regent
Street, called the Quadrant, was a covered way,
and nearly every other house was devoted to open
and public gambling. The same may be said of
Leicester Square. There was no limitation as to
the hours of closing places of entertainment, and
in many of these were exhibited the coarsest
description of vice. The saloons of the patent
theatres could not be entered by decent women.
Drunkenness exhibited itself in the foulest guise,

---

[1] In those days, one of the prisoners incarcerated in the Fleet
used to stand behind an opening and solicit alms from the passers-by;
his words were, 'Pray remember the poor debtors.'

and extended to classes now generally above its influence.

Clubs were comparatively few and not accessible to the masses, and taverns, amongst which I may mention the London Coffee House, on Ludgate Hill, and the Piazza, in Covent Garden, were still used by gentlemen of position and fashion. A restaurant had never been heard of, and would probably have been denounced as savouring of Bonaparte. *À la mode* beef-shops and eating-houses of different grades, but of little pretensions, furnished the entertainment necessary to those who could not enjoy the domestic dinner. One was in Rupert Street, called Hancock's, where excellent fare was provided at a very moderate rate, and served by the neatest of waitresses; and there were two French houses, called the Sablonnière and Newton's. The former, in Leicester Square, was supposed to represent the highest order of French cookery. Ladies were not admitted into any places of this class. The small houses in by-streets, in the City especially, with sanded floors, a fire, a gridiron, and a cook at the end of the room, the broiling hot steak or chop, the appetising kidney and sausage, are almost things of the past. Supper-houses, frequented only by men, were very important features of the night, and, if they reflected truly the tastes and manners of the generation, it would not be considered refined.

I may mention Evans's, the Coal Hole, the Cider Cellars, and Offley's. The suppers served were excellent, and, in addition, there was singing, the *habitués* sitting at the same table with the singers.

There were some good songs excellently sung, but there were others of a degrading and filthy character. Most of my readers will remember a scene described by Thackeray in his novel of ' The Newcomes,' referring to this subject, which is far more graphic and powerful than any I can attempt. It seems strange that in places undoubtedly frequented by gentlemen, obscenities of this description should have been encouraged ; but it must be remembered that in those days there were many coarse features throughout society.

Vice, clothed in its most repulsive garb, stalked publicly through the streets. Pugilism, treated as a noble English institution, created an atmosphere of coarseness and slang, and even in private society toasts were given and conversation was tolerated that would now shock the least refined.

There was one song sung, or rather recited, that made a considerable impression upon my mind, called ' Sam Hall.' The name of the singer was Ross. He had been an actor at several minor theatres.

The profanity of its expressions prevents my quoting the words. It was supposed to describe an interview between a condemned criminal and the Ordinary, whose well-intentioned advice is met by the felon with an account of his career, starvation, the gutter, cruelty, small theft, the corruption of a gaol, the brand upon him, robbery from a shop and the brutal sentence ;—the hopelessness of his entire life was most dramatically, and I think truly, portrayed. Before quitting the supper rooms I will venture to record a painful incident that occurred in connection with one of them. I had been to a ball at Kensington, and, together with some friends, went into the Cider Cellars to sup. Amongst them was a gentleman much valued by all of us, named Darrell Stephens. Whilst we were consuming kidneys and Welsh rarebits with all the vigour of youthful appetites, he was unmercifully chaffed for confining himself to a poached egg. Poor fellow ! he dropped down dead when walking in Fetter Lane the following day.

.I never witnessed any prize fights ; but the eloquent pen of Mr. Dowling surrounded them with a halo of glory. Spring and Langham, to my mind, appeared modern Ivanhoes, and the scene of encounter another field of Ashby-de-la-Zouch.[1] I

---

[1] See Appendix. I do not include the two I have mentioned in my subsequent description.

have, however, since witnessed some of these heroes enjoying their laurels, the deities of sporting pot-houses, where, with distorted noses, and an absence of the proper complement of teeth, eyes uncomfortably bunged up, and mouths reeking with gin, they were probably recording their former triumphs. I wonder whether it is true that the paladins of old, who are supposed to have leaped so gracefully on to their gallant steeds, and performed such miracles of valour in the prize fights of those days, were, in fact, lifted upon their chargers, and, when rolled off, frequently smothered in their iron mantles.

Periodical literature, which has now reached such gigantic dimensions, was then confined within comparatively small limits : the ' Edinburgh ' and the ' Quarterly ' were the only reviews ; ' Blackwood,' modestly calling itself a magazine, was supported by articles both grave and amusing ; ' Fraser ' introduced Thackeray to the public, and the ' Yellowplush Papers ' have never been surpassed, even by himself ; Theodore Hook rollicked in the ' New Monthly ' ; whilst Captain Marryat, in the pages of the ' Metropolitan,' detailed adventures and humorous scenes of sea life.

The ' Times,' conducted with wondrous ability, had become a director of public opinion, and there was scarcely a respectable household that did not secure a pennyworth of it in the course of the day, the price of which was sevenpence, precluding to many its entire purchase. Penny papers were unknown and undreamt of. In the middle classes five o'clock was an ordinary dinner hour ; and six o'clock was fashionable in the rare event of a party. *Menus* had not been heard of, and a dinner *à la Russe* had not travelled from the north. Paterfamilias presided over the food, and a perspiring carver did not dig lumps of meat from the joint and hand them with half cold gravy to the guests. It is a great mistake of dinner-givers in modern style to have joints at all : they are invariably carved in the most sickening fashion, and, from the appearance presented by the parts that reach the guests, might belong to any animal ever created.

I have in the foregoing pages given the reader some of the memories of the past, and my reflections thereon. There are others that I may hereafter record, which belong to a somewhat later period of my life, but I think it time to say something of those matters that more particularly belong to my professional career, and I therefore propose in my next chapter to introduce my readers to its commencement.

CHAPTER III.

COMMENCEMENT OF MY PROFESSIONAL LIFE.

I COMMENCED legal operations upon a second floor at No. 5 Inner Temple Lane—the same lane in which Dr. Johnson flourished. They were grimy old buildings then: their names even have ceased to exist, and handsome edifices fill up the space thus left. Dirt seemed at that time an attribute of the law. Now appearances are changed, and the surface is, at all events, much improved. In those days the evenings were supposed to be occupied by study, and consultations were held: now, after dark, passengers may seek in vain for the glimmer of a rushlight.

I cannot say that I burnt much midnight oil. No attorney, late from the country, ever routed me out and thrust a heavy brief into my hands— a circumstance which we have heard has so often been the origin of success to eminent lawyers. My establishment was limited. I shared with some half-dozen other aspirants to the Bench what, in Temple parlance, is called a laundress, probably from the fact of her never washing anything. I fancy that her principal employment was walking from my chambers to the pawnbroker's, and thence to the gin-shop. At the end of a short period my property, never very extensive, was reduced to little more than a pair of sheets, a teapot, and a coalscuttle, over which last it pleased Providence that she should tumble downstairs, and the injuries then sustained relieved me from her future attendance. A mischievous little urchin cleaned my boots, and was called clerk.

My means were extremely limited, and it may interest my readers to know what my professional earnings were during the first three years of my career. I was called to the bar in June, having attained the mature age of twenty-one the preceding March. Between that period and the following Christmas I made four guineas and a half; the second year I made thirty guineas, and the third seventy-five. I am afraid I must admit that I did not measure my expenditure by my income. My father had undertaken to furnish my chambers, and one of the principal articles he sent me was a horsehair arm-chair with only three legs, upon which I got so accustomed to balance myself that I scarcely felt safe on one furnished with the proper complement. He also had promised certain assistance by way of income, upon which promise I lived; but it was something like the income allowed to the Hon. Algernon Percy Deuceace by his father the Right Hon. the Earl of Crabs, recorded in the veritable History of Mr. Yellow-plush. I possessed one confiding tradesman. His name was Gill, he lived close by in Essex Court, and, fortunately for me, dealt in almost every article. My transactions with him remind me of a conversation recorded between a foreign prince and his steward. The former, complaining that his horses looked thin, was informed that the corn dealer would supply them with no more oats. ' Who will trust us ? ' asked the prince. After deep and long consideration the steward said that he thought they still had credit with the pastry-cook. ' Feed the horses upon tarts ! ' said the prince.

Gill was my resource for everything, from pats of butter to blacking. At last, after long suffering, he struck, shaking his head when I told him of the clients I expected. On the afternoon after this event I was balancing myself upon my three-legged chair in melancholy mood, and won-dering whence my dinner would come, when a knock sounded at my door, and a clerk from Messrs. Gilby and Allen,[1] blessed be their names! brought me, and paid for, three half-guinea motions. With this mine of wealth in my pocket ·I determined to enjoy myself luxuriously, and

[1] These gentlemen were well-known solicitors in Carlisle Street, Soho Square, and almost my earliest clients.

accordingly went to Hancock's, an establishment I have already described. The glorious repast still remains imbedded in my memory—twice of saddle of mutton; I am afraid to say how many helps of jam tart. After a handsome honorarium of threepence to Mary, who had never looked coldly upon me in my worst hours of impecuniosity, I had still twenty-five shillings left.

Wretch that I was, I forgot the patient Gill, and found my way into one of those sinks of iniquity, a gambling-house, in Leicester Square, and came out possessed of thirty-five pounds!

I was a millionaire. Gill once again smiled upon me, and the penny roll and pat of butter upon my breakfast table next morning testified to his restored confidence.

When I was called to the bar the police magistrates were qualified to sit upon the sessions bench, and the county justices might preside at the police offices, which they frequently did. My father on some occasions presided at the Middlesex Sessions. The smaller class of criminals were tried before this tribunal; there was also a large amount of civil business, consisting of poor-law appeals. These involved intricate points of law, and a great deal of money was spent in ridiculous contests ' between parishes in relation to the support of paupers. Mr. Bodkin, who afterwards became chairman, or, as it was then called, assistant-judge of these sessions, was an extremely able advocate in this kind of case, and from his early experience possessed much practical knowledge.

Mr. Clarkson, at first his usual antagonist, contrived to blunder through them, but he and others shortly yielded to Mr. Huddleston, afterwards and now a Baron of the late Exchequer, and one whose mind was of an order peculiarly qualified to master the technicalities of this description of business. This gentleman was one of my earliest friends at the bar. He possessed qualities which made his success only a matter of time. He was fond of society, but never neglected work, and his thorough knowledge of his causes made him a most powerful and efficient advocate.

His career has been in all respects a successful one, and there are few men who are able to reflect as he can that, both in public and in private life, he has attained every object of an honourable ambition. Whilst dwelling upon the Middlesex Sessions, I must say a few words of that curious-looking figure usually seated at the corner of the barrister's bench. One who saw him for the first time might be inclined to ask, What is it? Upon minute investigation might be discovered, encased in clothes far too large for him, the gaunt figure of a very unclean-looking man.

This was Mr. Michael Prendergast—'Mike,' he was always called. Slovenly as his dress was, his mind was more so : with a greater fund of general knowledge than most people, it seemed mixed so inextricably in his brain that it was next to useless. He rarely had any but the smallest cases from the dirtiest of clients, and whilst one of them was being tried would not unfrequently sit in a state of abstraction, out of which an unhappy clerk had to wake him. He possessed, however, much power at times, and great independence. I remember a little scene which will illustrate his habits not incorrectly. A case of his had been called on. He was late, and it was half over before he arrived in court—his clerk in an agony, the chairman grumbling. Of this, however, he took no notice whatever. 'Frederick' (to his clerk), 'where's my brief?' Loud whisper from Frederick, 'I gave it you in at breakfast: feel in your pockets.' A search commenced, and having first pulled out of his trousers' pocket a half-round of buttered toast, from the depths of it was extracted the single greasy sheet that constituted his instructions.

He was elected by the Court of Common Council to the small debts court in the City. How he managed the business there I have no means of knowing, but I am certain that he did so in the strictest spirit of justice.

The habits of the metropolis, which I have briefly sketched in the last chapter, furnished a class of business that occupied a considerable portion of time. Although, as I have already mentioned, gambling-houses of every degree were publicly open in many of the West End streets and squares, and although at this period they were not interfered with by the police or other authorities, they were illegal, and liable to indictment, and there was a nest of scoundrels who lived upon them. The great field for their operations was the Middlesex Sessions, and the Grand Jury their hunting-ground. Indictments were prepared, and true bills having been obtained, warrants were applied for, and granted as a matter of course. Armed with these, communications were opened with the keepers of the houses, some of whom, being wealthy, did not relish the prospect of twenty-four hours in prison before they would be admitted to bail, which was the first screw put on, and so these pillagers of the public had to submit to be pillaged themselves, and large sums of money were thus obtained. If these proceedings had been confined to the proprietors of such establishments, people would be inclined to say, let the thieves pick each other's pockets; but the trade was too profitable to be limited, and many instances occurred in which perfectly innocent people were made the victims of extortion by these harpies. Mr. Serjeant Adams, when he became chairman, put his foot upon their operations, by preventing warrants from issuing except under certain restrictions.

One of the worthies, who was a large proprietor of gambling-houses, became the lessee of the Adelphi Theatre, and Charles Phillipps used to relate an anecdote of his once meeting him and being offered a box, which he declined, thinking that some time or other he might be asked in return to defend the generous donor for nothing, and if Mr. Phillipps ever committed an irregularity, it certainly was not of that description. He asked him, however, how he was getting on. ' Capitally,' said the gentleman ; ' Providence seems to watch over all my undertakings.'

There was one great field-day held at the Middlesex Sessions, from which every member of the bar had the chance of picking up a guinea or two. This was the day appointed for hearing applications for music and dancing licences. Unless some complaint was made by the police, those that had previously existed were granted, as a matter of course ; but about the new ones there was generally a contest, certain of the justices taking the opportunity of ventilating what they called their ideas. A certain section of these gentlemen, none of them of position or note, opposed the grant to any of the applicants. A homily upon morals, the profanity of music, the indecency of dancing, and the length of ladies' dresses, formed the staple of their orations. Broad views upon what may fairly be deemed an important social question could not be expected from the speakers, and certainly never made their appearance. As far as I have been able to judge, assuming the perfect honesty of their worships, they betrayed simply a narrow-minded, unreasoning bigotry. One thing may be said of them, that, although their speeches rendered the tribunal ridiculous, they produced no other effect, as the result had been usually secured by a previous canvass. It seems to be time when these matters should be made subject to police regulation : it is manifestly most unjust that the interests of individuals, and the comforts and amusements of the people, should be regulated by the crotchets of a clique or the favouritism of a majority.

There existed another source of profit to the bar in connection with the magistracy. This arose from applications to local benches for the grant of spirit licences. Those not in the secret will scarcely believe what a licence was worth; and if there was not a considerable amount of jobbery about their disposition, all I can say is that the justices must have been an uncommonly pure body of men. Brewers and builders were the real

proprietors of many of the houses applied for—I
need hardly say in the names of nominees. I should
think that in some cases their value would ex-
ceed 3,000*l.* to 4,000*l.* The justices had been to
view the premises, elaborate plans were prepared,
learned arguments upon the state of the neighbourhood and the necessity for further accommodation were advanced. On the other hand, the
publicans already licensed rushed in a body to
oppose the grant : there was no traffic, there was
no custom, they and their families were starving.
It was amusing to look at the rosy countenances
of the starving publicans.

The justices, seated round a table in solemn
conclave, listened patiently to all that was said.
Spectacles upon respectable noses assisted in the
examination of the plans ; the rhetoric of counsel
was listened to with kindly attention. The chairman states that it is an important question, and
has been so ably argued on both sides that they
would like to consider it in private. The room is
cleared, every one knows how it is to go, except,
perhaps, a confiding client who may have hope
from the eloquent address of his advocate. This,
however, was a rare phenomenon. The justices
return, and announce the decision. I wonder, as
Cicero did of the augurs of his day, that they did
not burst out laughing in each other's faces.

I need not say that there were many distinguished names amongst the Middlesex magistracy,
but the possessors of them rarely, if ever, expressed
their views at the great ' October meet,'[1] or were to
be found at the different local licensing meetings.[2]

---

[1] The sessions for the grant and renewal of licences takes place in
this month.

[2] In the chapter in which I have endeavoured to sketch the state
of the streets of London in the days of my pupilage, I have given
them a character for coarseness and indecency, from which it may be
inferred that there is now a great improvement. I regret to say that
this is far from being the case. Scenes are now nightly enacted in
some of the principal thoroughfares of this metropolis that in a future
age will scarcely be credited. The coarseness, impurity, and vulgarity
of London appear to be massed within these localities.

CHAPTER IV.

MY EARLY PERFORMANCES.

It was at the sessions, of which in my last chapter I have given a brief account, that I made my first forensic display. The occasion was not an important one, nor productive of much profit.

I was instructed by a gentleman named Conquest to apply for the renewal of his licence, for a theatre called the Garrick, situated in Leman Street, Whitechapel. This place of amusement was within my father's district, who was then a magistrate of the Thames police, and it was probably from this circumstance that so much confidence was reposed in me. I rose, but could see nothing; the court seemed to turn round, and the floor to be sinking. I cannot tell what I asked, but it was graciously granted by the bench.

For this performance I received half a guinea, the sweetest that ever found its way into my pocket. Mr. Conquest, in addition to being the proprietor of this theatre, was a favourite low comedian, and very popular with the denizens of

the East. Another great favourite was Mr.
Gomersal, who, however, became better known
at Astley's Ampitheatre by his impersonation of
Napoleon Bonaparte in the drama of the 'Battle
of Waterloo.' An additional attraction at the
Garrick Theatre was the wife of the proprietor,
a very pleasing and pretty actress, and celebrated
as a ballet mistress, in which capacity she prepared many successful artistes for the stage. Mr.
Conquest migrated to the City Road, and for many
years managed the Eagle Saloon and Theatre with
credit and success. A son of his subsequently conducted it. He also was, and is an actor, and now,
I believe, delights the audiences of the Surrey
Theatre.

My diffidence had somewhat abated, when I
was entrusted with a brief by a rather shady
attorney of the Jewish persuasion; and being at
that time without experience, I yielded implicitly
to his instructions. A young gentleman of the
same faith was called as a witness. My client suggested a question. Blindly I put it, and was met
by a direct negative. 'What a lie!' ejaculated
my client, and dictated another question: the
same result followed, and a similar ejaculation.
By his further instruction I put a third, the answer
to which completely knocked us over. My client
threw himself back: 'Well,' said he, 'he is a liar,

he always was a liar, and always will be a liar.'
' Why,' remarked I, ' you seem to know all about
him.' ' Of course I do,' was the reply, ' he is my
own son ! '

Nothing struck me in my early days as more
odd than the number of different surnames in
which the same family of Jews seemed to delight.
One son of Mr. Saul Yales, of St. Mary Axe, was
Mr. Sidney, another Mr. Daniel, whilst a third re-
joiced in the appellation of Jacobs. I forget by
what names my client and his hopeful progeny
were known.

A gentleman of the name of Const presided as
chairman of the sessions when I joined them. He
was a friend of my father, and I received from
him all the encouragement he could give me.
Messrs. Charles Phillipps and William Clarkson, to
both of whom I shall have again to refer, did the
principal criminal business, and looked with no
friendly glances upon new-comers. Their greediness
for fees was an opprobrium to the court. Wrangles
constantly occurred, in which all sense of shame
seemed to be abandoned. The latter of the gentlemen I have named was under great obligations to
my father, but from neither of them did I ever
receive an act of kindness, or, until I had forced
my own way, barely of courtesy.

I may here mention a circumstance in which

I was the innocent cause of a sad catastrophe that happened to two of my clients. These were west-country farmers, who had been convicted of cruelty to animals, and had appealed from the conviction to the sessions. The question raised was as to the mode of conveying calves to market. Upon the day when the case should have been heard, I obtained a postponement to suit my convenience, and it came on the following week, when my clients were completely exonerated and the conviction was quashed.

They were returning home the same afternoon by the Great Western Railway, when a boiler burst. A mass of iron was projected into the air and fell upon the carriage in which they were seated, alighting between the two and killing them both.

Although the state of the streets was greatly improved by the institution of the new police, the gambling establishments still flourished. Leicester Square, the Quadrant, Bennett Street, Bury Street, and Duke Street were full of them. No concealment was affected. They were open to all comers, who were at some of them ushered in by powdered footmen. I learnt a great deal of the proceedings of these establishments from cases in which I was engaged at different times for and against the proprietors, and I believe that in most of these hells the chances of gain were assisted by flagrant trickery. At some of the principal—those, for instance, in Bennett Street—the decorations of the rooms were very elegant. Perfect quiet and decorum were observed by the players, who were generally of the better class.

The principal game played was hazard, of which there were two kinds : French hazard, in which the players staked against the bank, and English, or chicken hazard, in which they played against each other, with a settled profit to the proprietors. I fancy this mode of gambling was not so much exposed to fraud.

I do not think that rouge et noir was played anywhere. Roulette, which afforded abundant means of chicanery, was to be found at all the lower description of houses, and a game which seems now to be extinct, called ' une, deux et cinque.' This was played in a sort of basin lined with velvet, and a ball about the size of a cricket ball, with colours, red, black, and blue, as far as I can remember, stamped upon it. I cannot recollect how the game was played, but I was told that it was a fruitful means of cheating. With one example of the mode of procedure at roulette, through the medium of an accomplice, I became acquainted professionally. Most of my readers have seen a roulette table, and are aware that there are upon it thirty-six num-

bers, separated from each other by small divisions,
and that the players stake upon different numbers.
I need not recapitulate the way in which unwary
people were inveigled into these places. A class
of gentry called ' bonnets ' were actively engaged
in this employment : but when it was thought that
a good thing was on, the proprietor would say out
loud, ' We may as well be quiet : put up the bars.'
The intended victim supposed this to mean that
other people should be shut out, but the accomplice
took it as a direction to manipulate the table by
raising, which was done by machinery, an almost
imperceptible obstruction before any number which
would have secured to the player a large stake.
I was informed that most of the tables were so
constructed as to render this a very easy process.
The profits made must have been enormous.

The places, however, at which gambling might
be witnessed in all its magnitude, were the different racecourses. There might be seen a range
of booths, extending from the grand stand to the
end of the course, in all of which play in its various
forms, and at prices adapted to all classes, openly
flourished.

I have read that during the gold fever there
was not sufficient accommodation for the influx of
diggers within Melbourne, and that a quantity of
tents was erected outside the city. This was known

as the canvas town. The same term might have
been applied to the booths I have described, whilst
greed of gold was the distinctive emblem of both.

It was at one of these establishments that a
personage was pointed out to me who afterwards
became famous. He was a handsome-looking man,
with strongly marked Jewish features, and altogether not unprepossessing. This was Mr. Goodman, or Goody Levi, as he was usually called, twelve
years afterwards the hero of the Running Rein
fraud. It may bé remembered that he substituted
a four-year old horse called Maccabæus for Running Rein, and won the Derby with it. The fraud
was discovered, and upon a trial in the Court of
Exchequer before Baron Alderson fully exposed;
that learned judge, who was not wont to conceal
his opinions, observing that if gentlemen would
condescend to race with blackguards they must
expect to be cheated.

I noticed several well-known characters who
were patronising Mr. Goodman's, men who, when I
was young, were well known upon town. They
were all engaged in play: Count d'Orsay, the
dandy of the age, Lord Cantelupe, the Earl of
Chesterfield, and many others whom I have now
forgotten, and upon whom I then looked with
wonder and admiration.

The altar, however, at which the greatest sacrifices were made, and which reared its head above all rivals of a similar class, was that of which Mr. Crockford was the proprietor, and which went by his name. This was no mean refuge for everyday gamblers ; it was constituted as a club, and confined to members. It presented an imposing front on the upper part of the west side of St. James's Street. It is now, with little external alteration, the Devonshire Club. Personally I knew nothing of it, but heard romances of play related as having occurred within its precincts, of enormous sums changing hands, and of much sorrow and desolation invading many a family. Tales almost fabulous were related of its splendour, the luxuries that accompanied it, and of course of its orgies. I have always, however, heard that no suspicion of actual unfair play was entertained. The proprietor was himself a very large speculator upon the turf, and a story was told in connection with his death which, even if not true, shows the opinion that was entertained of the play fraternity of that day. It was said that he was very largely interested in a certain race, and that others following his lead had backed a particular horse that was considered likely to win. It is well known in the sporting world that if the maker of any bets dies before the event betted upon is determined the wagers are off. Mr. Crockford had been very ill, and much anxiety was felt

by the parties interested in the event. The horse
won ; but before the race the great speculator had
passed into another sphere. Those around him
are said to have kept this secret, and having learnt
by means of carrier pigeons the result of the race,
had supported his dead body in front of one of
the windows in St. James's Street, so that it might
be seen by the people returning from the course.
This may be a fable founded upon the character
of the persons concerned. It was generally believed, or, at all events, was generally asserted.

I heard from one of my disreputable acquaintances another curious story in connection with
the gambling sets, and about the truth of this
I entertain very little doubt. Names were given to
me, and circumstances related that strongly confirmed it : one or two of the persons are still living.
There were letter carriers employed by the Post
Office, who being in the pay of certain professional
betting men, regularly furnished them with information obtained from the letters of well-known
turfites, which they were in the habit of opening.
In those days envelopes were rarely used, and
letters written upon a sheet of paper were folded
and sealed ; by means of a kind of hook the sides
were extracted, and the contents could be de-
ciphered with tolerable accuracy.

He told me of one instance, giving me all the

names of the parties engaged. A person of very high position was the owner of a horse, which he had entered for a handicap race, and contrived by previous public trials of its speed to convey an inferior notion of the animal's powers, with a view to secure its being lightly weighted. This he communicated to people in his confidence, so that it might be backed at long odds; but the same knowledge having been previously obtained through the medium of the postman, the market had been used up, and his device, which was successful, turned to the profit of other more skilful but not greater rogues.

A man of middle age and middle height, clad in top boots and buckskin breeches, might on most Mondays and Thursdays be seen wending his way down Piccadilly. His goal was Tattersall's. This was Jem Bland, one of the greatest operators upon the turf. He could neither read nor write; he was ready, however, to make any number of bets, no matter of what amount. He could enter no memoranda, and no one entered any for him. But he had a most surprising memory, and upon returning to his house he dictated the list of his bets, with unfailing accuracy, to a lady connected with his establishment.

She also read all the letters addressed to him, and thus obtained a considerable amount of private

information of turf doings. This, he discovered,
she was in the habit of imparting to some of her
favourite acquaintances. He was fully equal to
the occasion. A great race was about to be run—
I think The Colonel and Zinganee were the com-
petitors. He conveyed to his fair friend a batch
of false reports, the circulation of which enabled
him to make a very good book, and after that he
changed his amanuensis.

In one of the most foul haunts of the metropolis there used to congregate many men of exalted rank, and (with the exception, of course, of
the clergy) of all professions, with them mixed
evil-looking keepers of low gaming, and, probably,
of other houses, betting men, prize fighters,
and bullies. After the saloons of the patent
theatres had disgorged their contents, those who
had not met with friends found their way to
this den. Unlimited drink pervaded the establishment. It was known as the Piccadilly Saloon, and
occupied part of the site of the present Criterion
Theatre. I had not the means, and I hope not
the taste, to join in the orgies that went on ; but
I have upon two or three occasions visited the
place, and have a lively recollection of the scenes
enacted. No play, it is true, went on overtly ; but
there were harpies on the look out for the unwary,
whom they inveigled to neighbouring slums, and

there drugged, robbed, and perchance murdered them.

I could name many of those who, I believe, nightly frequented this Pandemonium, but it would serve no useful purpose. There were, however, two, both public characters, whom I saw upon the few occasions I was there, and who particularly attracted my notice. One was Sam Chifney, the well-known jockey of George IV.; the other was a police magistrate, who presided at a court in the north-west district, and who, I was told, frequently left the saloon only in time to administer justice to the drunken and profligate who came within his jurisdiction.

One night, or rather the early morning, later in date than the period to which I have hitherto been referring, a group of six men were congregated at one of the tables. I was not present, and it is from the relation of a spectator that I have gathered the following particulars. With one of the party I had a slight acquaintance, having met him at the Cider Cellars and Evans's. He was a gentleman-like, unpresuming, and inoffensive young man. This was a person of the name of Mirfin. His position was that of a linendraper, or assistant to one, in Tottenham Court Road. He and a man named Elliott, whom I understood to be a retired Indian officer, got into a squabble. Mirfin had been drinking, and scarcely knew what he was about. Suddenly the party rose and left the room. It seems that they obtained pistols, and the whole six, occupying two hackney coaches, drove to Wimbledon Common, and there a sad combination of farce and tragedy was performed. Poor Mirfin was put up and fired at by Elliott, an expert shot. Probably Mirfin himself had never handled anything more dangerous than a yard measure. The first shot went through his hat. He was plucky enough, however, for again he stood up to be fired at, and Elliott succeeded in murdering him.

The affair, from the brutality and ridicule that accompanied it, the circumstances that led to it, and the place in which the quarrel occurred, gave a finishing stroke to an institution already tottering ; and the assassins who, through the false shame of men of honour, were able to pursue a system of terrorism, are now infamies of a past generation in this country. In a neighbouring one the practice fortunately appears to be verging on the confines of burlesque.

CHAPTER V.

CHOICE OF CIRCUIT.

In former chapters I have brought my readers to
the period when it was necessary to choose my
course of proceeding in the legal struggle I was
about to commence, and my interests as well as
my finances pointed to the metropolitan and ad-
jacent districts. Accordingly, I joined the Middlesex Sessions, of which tribunal I have already
given some description, being introduced by a
gentleman named Alley, a leader of the bar.
Subsequently I joined the Central Criminal Court,
and almost as a consequence fixed upon the
Home Circuit, which consisted of Hertfordshire,
Essex, Sussex, Kent, and Surrey. In choosing
a circuit, a barrister, with certain exceptions,
is bound by his first choice, and it ought to
be made with grave deliberation. When I was
called there were no railways. We were not
allowed to use public conveyances or live at hotels.
The leaders generally travelled, accompanied by
their clerks, in their own carriages, the juniors

two or three together, in dilapidated post-chaises. It was customary for the judges to enter the town before the bar, and, as it is called, open the commission, after which they adjourned to church, affording a grand opportunity to the sheriff's chaplain, usually a very young man, to enforce upon them their duties as citizens and judges. During this ceremony the carriages came rattling in, lodgings were engaged, the juniors, two or three of them, sometimes more, occupying one sitting-room. The attorneys were to be seen hurrying with the briefs destined for their fortunate recipients, witnesses lounged about the bars of the public-houses, and the juniors wandered up and down the street wondering what they should do with themselves and whether a good time was coming.

The next morning (the commission was usually opened on a Monday) the real business of the assizes began. A flourish of trumpets, not necessarily in harmony, announced that His Majesty's judges would take their seats in half an hour, another flourish that they had done so: one in the Crown Court, the other in the Civil. The former court is the great object of attraction. A real judge is a sight to see; he is clad in scarlet; the High Sheriff, in a mysterious costume, sits beside him; solemnity is given to the scene by the presence of a parson. It is said that even the criminal is elated by a sense of the dignity of his position, so different from being tried by Squire Jones in his blue coat and drab trousers. I suspect, however, that the fact that the judge will not take into consideration his being a notorious poacher is in reality the cause of his satisfaction. His lordship, in charging the grand jury, probably congratulates them upon something, and remits them to perform the not very arduous duties of indorsing their own previous committals, that tribunal being principally composed of the magistrates of the county. The trials are then proceeded with, and disposed of with impartiality and decorum.

The criminal courts of the assizes give the junior members of the bar an opportunity of ventilating their powers, and they almost invariably receive assistance and encouragement from the judges. The feeling thus early engendered produces through a subsequent professional career the kindly intercourse that exists between bench and bar, in no respect derogating from the dignity of the former or the independence of the latter.

I remember the great French advocate, M. Berryer, remarking upon this trait of the profession in our country with some surprise, but with warm admiration.

In the meanwhile the business in the Civil

Court has commenced. There is a kind of inter-
lude of undefended causes. The court is densely
crowded by barristers, who, during the charge to
the grand jury, are excluded from the Crown
Court, lest they should hear what the judge
says, and take a hint from it. Of course if there
is anything useful to know, the solicitors, who are
not excluded, repeat it. This is an old-fashioned
absurdity, which ought to be abolished.

A cause is called on. The acceptance to a
bill of exchange not contested has to be proved.
A voice is heard from the middle of the crowd
enunciating with difficulty, 'May it please your
lordship——' 'Pray speak out,' says the judge.
The counsel almost collapses, but, struggling and
panting, at last succeeds in giving the necessary
proof, and so a number of cases are disposed of,
and the real business of the Civil Court commences.
The leaders have taken their seats, exchanged
bows with the judges, nodded to each other, and
the stereotyped dialogue ensues between the judge
and leader, 'On what day, Mr. ——, will it be
convenient to take special juries?' 'The bar is
at your lordship's disposal.' 'What do you
say to Thursday?' 'It will suit admirably.'
'Thursday be it then. Mr. Sheriff, let the special
juries be summoned for Thursday next.' And
now horses are off, and the day is exhausted

upon the trial of usually trifling causes. The adjournment at last arrives. The former opponents walk to their lodgings, chatting gaily together; and the juniors rejoice that the time has come when all meet at a dinner, where good-humour and thorough cordiality between the highest and the lowest in the professional scale usually reign. I will not run the risk of wearying my readers with any long description of the mess, but I think that I may mention, to the credit of its members, that no personal jokes prevailed, and though laughter was often excited at the expense of one or other of the members, it was thoroughly good-humoured. Officers were elected. An Attorney- and Solicitor-General brought offenders to justice. One offence was, going special to another circuit. It was one of gravity, and an exemplary fine was imposed. Getting married was passed over with a simple admonition, upon the ground that it carried its own punishment with it. There was a poet laureate, and sometimes the verses composed were amusing, and, if personal, without bitterness. Mr. Arnold, afterwards a judge in India, filled at one time this office with much credit. He was an accomplished poet as well as lawyer.

One of the means of extracting fun was making the criminal address the mess in aggravation of his offence. And I must here mention a gentle-man who will not appear in any of my strictly legal recollections, but whose memory will always be regarded by members of the profession, espe-cially those on the Home Circuit, with respect and affection.

John Locke, member for Southwark, now no more, was the very soul of the circuit table : his speeches elicited roars of laughter. I have often endeavoured to explain to myself in what particular attribute his humour consisted, but it was as little to be defined as it was impossible to resist. I have only met one instance of a some-what parallel character. This was in another valued friend, now also passed away, the late Mr. Sothern. In 'Lord Dundreary' he created, by means especially his own, the most uncontrollable laughter, and the same mystery, as in the case of John Locke, enveloped the cause.

The apparently utter confusion of mind, the striving vainly to get hold of the threads of a subject, the look of vacancy attending the failure, and the solemn attempt to resume the struggle, were features common to both. I recall these gentlemen as having furnished many of the most amusing hours of my life, and join with all their friends in mourning over their departure.

One other institution I must not omit to men-

tion—the dinner given by the judges to the bar,
at which young and old were kindly received. A
custom, now extinct, then existed of each guest
giving the judge's servants two shillings. This
gave rise to the entertainment being profanely
called a two-shilling ordinary. As trumpets
initiated the assizes, so they celebrated their ter-
mination. The rickety post-chaises were again
called into requisition, and in another town the
judges underwent the same trumpeting, and with
their last blast each town was left to slumber in
its pristine dulness.

When I joined the circuit Mr. Serjeant Spankie
and Mr. Serjeant Andrews were in a partial lead.
The former had held high office in India. I
scarcely remember him. The latter was possessed
of a very solemn appearance.

There were two members who both gave great
promise, and were looked upon as the future
leaders : one was Mr. Turton, who closed his career
in this country by accepting an appointment in
Calcutta ; the other, a Mr. Broderic, who succumbed
prematurely to ill-health.[1] These events left a
splendid opening for Mr. Thesiger, who ultimately
shared the lead with Mr. Platt. As is known, the

---

[1] I have no personal recollection of either of these gentlemen, but
my father, who remembered them both, has described the former to
me as possessing all the qualities of an accomplished advocate, and the
latter as a most acute and learned lawyer.

former passed through the offices of Solicitor- and
Attorney-General, and ultimately became Chancellor during Lord Derby's administration. He
received this post whilst conducting the prosecution of the British Bank directors, in which I
was associated with him, and I may say that
I never heard a finer effort than his opening of
the lengthy and complicated facts of that cause.
He was very painstaking and industrious. His
appearance was greatly in his favour—tall, with
well-marked and handsome features; his manner
was slightly artificial, and his jokes, of which he was
fond, were somewhat laboured. He had been when
a boy in the navy, and was, I have heard, in one of
Nelson's engagements. When called to the bar he
joined the Surrey Sessions, where he soon was deservedly held in high favour, and selected the Home
for his circuit. I do not think he was very popular when he became a leader. He was accused
of favouritism in giving references, and was surrounded by a clique who received them.[1] As an
advocate he was successful with special juries,
but Platt beat him before common ones. He was
eminently correct in his demeanour, and set an
excellent example to the bar by his regular attendance at the Temple Church. When Chancellor he
refused Serjeant Parry and myself, both of us in

---

[1] The selection of junior members of the bar to arbitrate becomes
very invidious when a leader selects only his own personal friends.

good business, patents of precedents, upon the
ground that he had fully made up his mind never
to confer that rank upon a serjeant. He afterwards very properly, but very inconsistently, conferred it upon Serjeant Simon and Serjeant Sargood. A great scandal was created by his ap-
pointing a near connection of his own Master in
Lunacy. This office was intended for lawyers
of standing and experience, and the gentleman in
question was only nominally a barrister, and held
a clerkship in some public office, and, although
possessing very high qualifications, certainly did
not come within the intention of the statute creating
the office. Mr. Disraeli, shocked at what had the
appearance of a job, declined to defend it in the
House of Commons. The gentleman selected instantly sent in his resignation, and Lord Chelmsford then appointed Samuel Warren, himself little
better than a lunatic, although a clever one.

Warren was, at the time, in the House of Commons, and pronounced a sort of funeral oration
upon himself when leaving it, which was listened to
with more patience and apparent satisfaction than
any of his former speeches. When Mr. Disraeli reformed the Conservative Government he left out.
Lord Chelmsford, and appointed Lord Cairns to
fill the office of Chancellor. One of this nobleman's acts was to raise Alfred Thesiger, a son

of Lord Chelmsford, to the post of Lord Justice. The appointment was considered premature ; but every one who knew Mr. Thesiger felt that his legal knowledge and indefatigable industry warranted the selection, whilst his unvarying courtesy and real kindness of heart disarmed unkind comments, and his early death caused universal regret in the profession and to all who knew him. I cannot forbear offering a personal tribute to his memory. He has been with me and against me in several cases ; most pleasantly we got on together, and the friendliness which I believe existed between us was by no means diminished by his promotion. I know of no one for whom I felt a more sincere regard.

During the period that I was what was humorously called reading at Watson's, my parents were still at Hampstead, and I became acquainted with a family who, from their connections and associations, were, as well as in themselves, extremely interesting. They consisted of grandmother, daughter, and grandson. The eldest of the three was Mrs. Denman, widow of the eminent physician ; the second lady was her daughter, also a widow. Her husband was the celebrated Sir Thomas Croft. It is well known that the young and popular Princess Charlotte died whilst under his care. Much bitterness existed at that time against her father, and calumnies extended very unjustly to his physicians. Sir Thomas was very sensitive, and his mind gave way under the pain inflicted. Sir Thomas Croft, their son, who had been in the Guards and fought at Waterloo, was frequently of the party, and it was through my acquaintanceship with them that I first knew Sir Thomas Denman, the son of Mrs. Denman, Lady Croft's brother and uncle of Sir Thomas. He was then Attorney-General, and came frequently to see his relatives, and through the length and breadth of the land a more truly affectionate and happy family never existed.

It is impossible for memory to dwell upon a more noble figure than that of the mother of the future Lord Chief Justice. Her features were strongly marked, and greatly resembled his when he had arrived at a later period of his life. They lived upon Heath Mount, where I was frequently received by them. Mrs. Denman was very fond of whist, and would play three or four rubbers without apparent fatigue.[1] The party consisted of the three I have already mentioned and myself. I think I remember Miss Joanna Baillie on one occasion joining the tea-table. They were

[1] At this period long whist was always played, and I imagine that old-fashioned people thought there was profanity in the change that at this time was only darkly hinted at.

all most kind to me, and, independent of the boon they conferred by making me known to the future Chief Justice, I shall always feel that their society was one of the most agreeable incidents of my life.

As I only profess to give my own experiences, and leave history to deal with general events, I have but little to record relating to Lord Denman's career. Every one has heard of the noble stand he made in defence of Queen Caroline, and it speaks well for William IV., upon whom during the trial he made a bitter attack, that it was by his appointment that he became Lord Chief Justice. Whilst he filled that office my practice was confined principally to the criminal courts, and consequently, except upon the occasions when he presided at those tribunals, I had no opportunity of observing him. His manner was uniformly gracious and kindly, and his demeanour dignified. Cruelty, or oppression of any kind, would elicit from him occasional bursts of indignation, but in his administration of criminal justice he never forgot the natural frailty of human nature.

One personal incident, having an important bearing upon my career, I may be permitted to mention. I had been just four years at the bar, and neither my prospects nor finances were flourishing. The spring assizes were going on at Maid-

stone, when one of the boatmen attached to the
Thames Police called on me, in great distress. His
mother was in grievous trouble. She had committed some small offence, and was to be tried before
Lord Denman. At the poor fellow's entreaty I defended her, and she was acquitted. At the judges'
dinner, afterwards, Lord Denman, shaking hands
with me, said, ' You did that case very well, but it
was the witnesses to character got the woman off.'
He alluded also to the meetings at his mother's of
which I have made mention. On the summer
assizes following he was also the judge, and I applied to him for a revising barristership. There was
only one vacancy, which he gave to a Mr. Kennedy.
I happened, in somewhat disconsolate mood, to go
into the court as it was rising, and caught his
eye. As I heard afterwards, after seeing me, he
sent for Montague Chambers, who held a revising
appointment, and asked him if his position upon
circuit was not such that he might dispense with it.
That gentleman at once placed it at Lord Denman's
disposal, and he sent it to me. The remuneration
was not large, but at that time it was vitally
serviceable. I held the appointment for four years,
when the number was diminished, and those
last appointed were excluded. My colleague upon
this occasion was Mr. Shee, afterwards a judge of
the Queen's Bench.

I am sure the members of my profession will excuse me for saying a few words on Chambers, and I believe all will join me in the tribute, that this opportunity gives me of paying, to one who not only served me on that occasion, but with whom I have always remained on terms of friendship. Originally in the Guards, he doffed the scarlet at the call of duty and affection, became an assiduous worker, a successful advocate, and leader of the Home Circuit, and no man ever attained position who, by strict honour, fairness, and integrity, deserved it better. I am glad to say that, although he has retired from the profession, I still meet him at a club to which we both belong ; and whilst he has not reaped the highest honours, he is always contented and in good spirits, and not altogether unwilling to furnish his numerous friends with some of the anecdotes of his career.

CHAPTER VI.

THE THAMES POLICE COURT.

AT the time I was called to the bar my father was a magistrate, and was residing at the official residence of the Thames Police, then situated at Wapping, on the river bank, opposite to what was called Execution Dock, where, but shortly before, it was the custom to hang pirates in chains. He had for a colleague an old sea captain of the name of Richbell. It was thought, in those days, that the experiences of navigating a ship on the sea would be a good preparation for administering the law in connection with the river. At this office there was a staff of police under the control of the magistrate, and the river was patrolled by this force. I was accustomed to accompany them day and night. They saved my limited resources the expense of cabs; and many is the chase I have joined in of suspicious wherries, and sometimes a scamper, not unattended with danger, upon shore, when the officers were in the performance of their duties. I believe them to have been an admirable body of men, joining discipline with much of the knowledge possessed by the old Bow-Street runners; and it was to one of these men that I was indebted for the brief that, as I have already mentioned, brought me to the attention of Lord Denman.

A Mr. Broderip became colleague with my father upon the decease of Captain Richbell. A barrister, a good lawyer, and refined gentleman, he was a fellow of the Zoological Society, and took great delight in the inmates of the Gardens. I cannot refrain from mentioning an anecdote that occurred many years after, when he had been transplanted to the Marylebone Police Court. I was then in some criminal practice, and appeared before him for a client who was suggested to be the father of an infant, and about which there was an inquiry. Mr. Broderip very patiently heard the evidence, and, notwithstanding my endeavours, determined the case against my client. Afterwards, calling me to him, he was pleased to say, ' You made a very good speech, and I was inclined to decide in your favour, but you know I am a bit of a naturalist, and while you were speaking I was comparing the child with your client, and there could be no mistake, the likeness was most striking.' ' Why, good heavens!' said I, ' my client was not in court. The person you saw was the attorney's clerk.' And such truly was the case.

My father afterwards took a house in Cadogan Place, where he died. I remember the late Charles Mathews canvassing him for his vote for the appointment of district surveyor at Bow. He obtained it, and also the place. Fancy one of the brightest of mortals amongst the chimney-pots of Bow! He did not long remain in this uncongenial sphere ; and I remember shortly after, in company with a large party, consisting of Adolphus and others, old and fast friends of his father, seeing him make his first appearance at the Olympic Theatre in the farce of 'Old and Young Stagers,' inaugurating the brilliant career which, to the sorrow of all acquainted with him, has recently terminated.

Mr. Const, who, as I have already mentioned, presided at the Middlesex Sessions when I joined them, occupied a house at the eastern corner of Clarges Street, in Piccadilly. He kept an open table for his intimate friends who were in the habit of notifying their intention to dine—within a certain number and up to a given hour of the day. My father was one of the privileged—and I was frequently received at these parties, where I met very pleasant people—amongst others, William Dunn, 'Billy Dunn'—treasurer of Drury Lane Theatre— and sometimes departed, after a hospitable dinner, with tickets in my pocket for Old Drury, no small boon to a pocket that did not contain much cash.

Sir Frederick Roe was also a constant and very welcome visitor. I believe that he succeeded Sir Robert Baker as chief magistrate at Bow Street. He was a tall, handsome, gentlemanly man, who had the reputation of having enjoyed life in many phases. He succeeded to a large fortune, and retired from the bench. I remember my father congratulating him upon his accession to wealth. 'Ah!' said he, with a deep sigh, 'it has come too late.'

A very different style of magistrate was Mr. Laing, whom I also frequently met. I never saw him without thinking of a shrivelled crab apple. In the story of 'Oliver Twist' Charles Dickens caricatured him under the name of Fang.

A reverend gentleman complained of him to the Home Office. I fancy he had exhibited some irritability of temper in a case before him, and the authorities were not sorry to follow the lead of a popular author, and dismissed him. His accuser was shortly afterwards convicted of stealing a silver spoon at a charity dinner at which he presided.

Mr. Laing, notwithstanding an unfortunate temper, was a thoroughly honourable gentleman, a good lawyer, and accomplished scholar, very precise in his dress, but, as I have said, very sour-looking. Every day of his life he might be seen at the same hour wending his way to the Athenæum Club, where he always dined.

I do not think that glibness and self-confidence
exhibited early in court are a good augury for ulti-
mate success. No one, until he has measured himself with others, has a right to form a high opinion
of himself. It is true that after a young barrister
has ejaculated with difficulty a few incoherent
words, he sits down with a parched throat, and
a sort of sickening feeling that he will never
succeed ; but the most successful of advocates have
experienced these sensations, and to this day I
believe that many rise to conduct cases of importance with some of their old emotions. In a
former chapter I have described my sensations
when first I was called upon to address the court,
and it was long before I could do so with any amount
of confidence.

Although in the legal scale criminal courts and
criminal trials do not hold the first places, they are
of far more importance in the eyes of the general
public than those tribunals and elaborate investigations by which the greatest reputations and highest
rewards are obtained, and the Crown courts ought
to be presided over by men who can command
and enforce respect. Such certainly was not the
rule when, in natural connection with the Middlesex Sessions, I first joined the bar at the Central
Criminal Court; and there can be no doubt that
the mode in which business was conducted in that

tribunal made it a term of opprobrium to be called
an Old Bailey barrister.   Except in very grave
cases, the business was presided over by judges
appointed by the City.   A canvass amongst a parcel
of by no means the highest class of tradesmen,
who were quite incompetent to form a judgment,
obtained for candidates the places of Common Serjeant and Commissioner, the Recorder being appointed by the Court of Aldermen.   The sittings of
the court commenced at nine o'clock in the morning, and continued until nine at night.   There were
relays of judges.   Two luxurious dinners were provided, one at three o'clock, the other at five.   The
Ordinary of Newgate dined at both.   The scenes
in the evening may be imagined, the actors in them
having generally dined at the first dinner.   There
was much genial hospitality exercised towards the
bar, and the junior members were given frequent
opportunities of meeting the judges and other
people of position ; but one cannot but look back
with a feeling of disgust to the mode in which
eating and drinking, transporting and hanging,
were shuffled together.

The City judges rushing from the table to take
their seats upon the bench, the leading counsel scur-
rying after them, the jokes of the table scarcely
out of their lips, and the amount of wine drunk, not
rendered less apparent from having been drunk

quickly—this is now all changed. The early dinners and evening sittings have been interred with
other barbarisms, and the hours are the same as in
the civil courts. At the period I am speaking of,
Mr. Cotton was the Ordinary—not easily to be
forgotten, somewhat tall, very portly. His rubicund visage betokened the enjoyment of the good
things of this life. He was most punctual in his
attendance at both dinners, and never affronted the
company by abstinence at either. He possessed a
sort of dry humour, and I fancy was popular in the
City. I had no opportunity of learning whether
he performed the very different offices connected
with his appointment with the same success that he
did his prandial ones. One of the jokes recorded
of him has often been repeated. It was part of his
duty to say grace, including in it a prayer for the
principal officials. ' Why,' he was asked, ' do you
not name the under-sheriffs? ' ' I only pray for
great sinners,' was his reply.

The Honourable Charles Ewan Law, whom I
have already mentioned, was the Recorder: dignified
in manner before dinner always, and merciful, pompous, and disagreeable, he possessed ability quite
equal to the necessities of his office. I remember
an amusing incident connected with him. On one
occasion, after dinner, he overturned his tray of
coffee, which was resting upon the bench. He said

not a word.   The same jury sat the next morning.
He had some coffee brought in—quite an unusual
thing at that hour.   Somehow it went over, to the
great discomfiture of the Clerk of Arraigns, who sat
underneath. Turning to the jury, he said : ' Gentlemen, I have constantly begged that the desk
should be made broader. I met with the same
accident on another occasion.' Mirehouse, the
Common Serjeant, always called Taffy, was a hot-
headed Welshman, good-humoured and kindly
enough.   He turned the court into a low-comedy
theatre.   Arabin, the Commissioner, a shrewd,
quaint little man, enunciated absurdities with most
perfect innocence.

   'I assure you, gentlemen,' he said one day to
a jury, speaking of the inhabitants of Uxbridge,
' they will steal the very teeth out of your mouth as
you walk through the streets.   *I know it from experience.*' It ought to be mentioned, to the credit
of the Corporation, that it had upon a former occasion elected Mr. Denman as Common Serjeant,[1] and
the most pleasant years I passed in the court were
during the time that the Honourable James Stuart
Wortley was Recorder. This gentleman was an excellent judge, and extremely popular with everybody.[2]

---

   [1] This was before my time.
   [2] He afterwards became Solicitor-General, and was succeeded by
Mr. Gurney.

On a morning in October 1834 I was entertained at breakfast in the Regent's Park. A tall, gaunt old gentleman was my host. Afterwards I was taken down in a most respectable family coach to the Sessions House, Clerkenwell Green, and there introduced to my future companions at the bar. Mr. Alley, as I have before mentioned, one of its oldest members performed this kindly office. He had had formerly a large business in the criminal courts, sharing it mainly with Mr. Adolphus; but both these gentlemen were now succumbing to the inroads of younger men, Charles Phillipps and Clarkson, with Bodkin bringing up the rear, getting the cream of the business. Peter Alley was an Irishman; he had the reputation of being a good criminal lawyer, and although his manners were rough, his feelings were those of a gentleman. He was most hospitable and kind. I have already mentioned a well-known tavern called the London Coffee House. It still exists, but its character is changed. Then it was frequented by merchants and City men of position, and during the sittings of the Central Court, Alley used to dine there often, and invited from time to time members of the bar, to whom the dinner was both an object and a compliment. I was many a time his guest. He and Adolphus had numerous quarrels, one of which led to the oft-recorded duel on the Calais Sands. I have heard a

story in connection with it which is rather amusing.
I imagine that neither of them wanted to fight; but
after one of these disputes, Adolphus sent a letter
of the most insulting character to Alley's house. He
might have addressed it to his chambers. By accident, of course, Peter left the letter on the table,
where Mrs. Alley found it, and, naturally, also read
it.   Alley blamed his carelessness bitterly ; but his
wife, having true Hibernian blood in her veins,
holding the missive in her hands, exclaimed, ' Peter,
much as I love you, I would sooner see you brought
home on a stretcher than submit to such an insult.'
The two fought, and one, I forget which, shot off a
part of the other's ear.   They were both very proud
of the exploit, and, with a few growls, remained
afterwards tolerable friends.   Let me say a few words
of Adolphus.   He was nearly a great man, and but
for an unfortunate temper would probably have
risen to the highest honours of the profession.   He
was a lucid and impressive speaker, and possessed
a singularly logical mind.   A fair judgment may
be formed of his powers by reading a speech he
made upon the Cato Street conspiracy case, in
which he greatly distinguished himself.

He was called to the bar at a comparatively
late stage of life, and although occasionally engaged in civil causes, remained almost to the day
of his death a practitioner in the criminal courts

During some portion of the period when he was in practice, Tenterden, a morose judge, who was supposed to be much under the influence of Sir James Scarlett, was Chief Justice of the Queen's Bench.

Sir James upon one occasion, how provoked I do not know, said, 'Mr. Adolphus, we are not at the Old Bailey.' 'No,' was the response, 'for there the judge presides and not the counsel.'[1] When I first knew Adolphus he had attained an advanced age, and it was sad to witness the wreck he had become; sad to think of a life so wasted, of great abilities so cast away. There was little generosity shown him by those who were at this time doing the principal business; and pigmies to him in intellect were enabled, through his unhappy irritability, to drive him almost to madness.[2] Whilst referring to his temper, I am pleased to record that to his juniors and his inferiors it was never exhibited. To them he was unvaryingly considerate and kind; and I must also mention that he had been for years a sufferer from a painful disease, which he bore with the greatest patience and magnanimity. He lived in Gower Street, where he gave frequent parties, which were very popular,

---

[1] Since writing the above, I have met the anecdote differently worded in Campbell's *Lives of the Chief Justices.*

[2] These observations do not include Mr. Bodkin.

mainly through the accomplishments of his daughter and daughter-in-law, the wife of his only son, John Leycester Adolphus, afterwards a county court judge. He himself was a thorough-going Tory, and wrote a history of George III. through Tory glasses, and when he died, an affectionate father and sincere friend passed away.

Mr. Charles Phillipps was a curious compound of intellectual strength and weakness. He was master of undoubted genius, and power of speech amounting at times to eloquence, but was deficient in moral courage and self-reliance. He was an Irishman by birth, and his face and figure were greatly in his favour—tall, with well-formed and expressive features, and a musical voice. He had commenced his career on the Munster Circuit, where he produced a great impression upon juries more impulsive than those he had to address in England. Several specimens are given of his style by a gentleman who has written some very amusing articles in a magazine which until lately was called the ' Dublin University.' He was still young when he came over to this country, and, somewhat inflated by the praises he had obtained, imagined himself to possess all the attributes, instead of only the more superficial ones, of a great orator. Wanting in discretion when before a tribunal of which he had no experience, he laid himself open to a merciless attack at the hands of Brougham in one of the first cases in which he appeared in the Court of Queen's Bench. He collapsed under the punishment, and rarely appeared afterwards in any of the civil courts. A romantic incident occurred at the commencement of his residence in this country, in the shape of a love-affair with a very beautiful girl, whom he subsequently married, and a duel with an unsuccessful rival.

When I commenced my career he was signally the prisoners' counsel at the Old Bailey, the Middlesex Sessions, and also upon the Oxford Circuit. In this capacity he was certainly at that time unrivalled. He had great readiness, a power of repartee, earnestness when it was required; and whatever deficiency he may have shown in his earlier career, he had acquired a very sound judgment. He was never dull, and the juries liked him. I remember upon one occasion, in the robing-room, when poor Adolphus, in a state of irritation, and when his business had nearly all fallen into the hands of Phillipps, said to that gentleman : 'You remind me of three B's—Blarney, Bully, and Bluster;' 'Ah!' said Phillipps, 'you never complained of my B's until they began to suck your honey.'

I may here mention an incident that occurred in connection with the trial in which Brougham

and Phillipps were opposed, and which I believe to be perfectly true. A friend of the latter
gentleman, of the name of MacDowell, was a re-
porter upon the staff of the 'Times' newspaper,
and it fell to his lot to report his friend's speech.
The reply of Brougham came within the province
of another gentleman. MacDowell wished his associate to leave out some of the more stinging passages, but he would not be persuaded to swerve
from his duty. MacDowell contrived, however, to
soften their effect by omitting the parts in Phillipps's
speech to which they referred, and, this being discovered, he lost his position on the 'Times.'

My father, from whom I heard the story, knew
the poor fellow, who never afterwards rallied, and
died, I fear, in great poverty. Phillipps himself
kissed the rod that had chastised him and became
a constant associate of Lord Brougham, who,
when Chancellor, made him Commissioner of Bank-
ruptcy at Liverpool, an office for which he was
singularly unfitted. Subsequently he was appointed
to be one of the judges of the old Insolvent Court,
which required a good knowledge of figures, about
which he knew nothing; and his colleague, who
knew little more, was a gentleman notoriously more
insolvent than most of the suitors who sought relief
at his hands.

CHAPTER VII.

THE TRIAL OF COURVOISIER.

SHORTLY before Mr. Phillipps left the bar his name
became associated with the Courvoisier trial, which
for many reasons interested me, and some of the
circumstances of which may, I think, equally interest my readers.

On April 6, 1840, Lord William Russell was
found murdered at his house, No. 14 Park Lane.
London was in a state of excitement. The age
of the nobleman, his great historic name, and
position in society, all combined to aggravate the
horror naturally excited by such an event. The circumstances clearly pointed to domestic treachery;
and Courvoisier, his confidential valet, was apprehended, and, on June 18 following, was put upon
his trial, charged with the murder. The occasion
might, from the appearance the Old Bailey presented, have been thought one of the most festive
character. The court was crowded with ladies
dressed up to the eyes, and furnished with lor-
gnettes, fans, and bouquets; the sheriffs and under-
sheriffs, excited and perspiring, were rushing here

and there, offering them what they deemed to be
delicate attentions. A royal duke honoured the
exhibition with his presence, and, upon the occasion of a witness giving a particular answer to a
question from counsel, showed his approval by an
ejaculation of ' Hear, hear.'

Sir Nicholas Tindal, the presiding judge, was
so hemmed in by the extensive draperies of the
surrounding ladies that he had scarcely room to
move, and looked disgusted at the indecency of the
spectacle; and I may here say that the scenes still
occasionally presented upon celebrated trials at the
Old Bailey do little credit to the officials who en-
courage them. Mr. Baron Parke, to whom I shall
hereafter allude, was associated with the Chief
Justice upon the trial. Mr. Adolphus led for the
prosecution, and in opening it made allusions,
scarcely in good taste, to the fact of the accused
being a foreigner, giving Mr. Phillipps, who defended him, an opportunity for a display of eloquent
protest. The trial lasted for three days; and the
proceedings upon the two first were scarcely conclusive enough to have secured the conviction.
Upon the third day, when I came into the robing-
room in the morning, I found Mr. Phillipps there,
evidently very much agitated. I learnt afterwards
that some new evidence of an important character
had come to the knowledge of the prosecution and
been communicated to him.

A considerable quantity of plate had disappeared from Lord William's house, and it was discovered that immediately after the murder it had been deposited by Courvoisier with some people in the neighbourhood of Leicester Square. This circumstance had been disclosed on the previous evening. Courvoisier, to whom it was made known, requested an interview with his counsel, which was very properly accorded, and upon this occasion he admitted the correctness of the statement as to the discovery.

He did not, as was generally supposed and asserted at the time, avow that he had committed the murder, although doubtless what he did own was very stringent evidence of the fact; and the communication was certainly made, not for the purpose of admitting his guilt, but merely to prepare his counsel to deal with the evidence.

The course pursued by Mr. Phillipps showed the inherent weakness of his character. It was peculiarly a situation for self-reliance and sound judgment. He was bound to continue the defence ; although no doubt his mode of conducting it could not but be materially affected by the new circumstances. Mr. Phillipps, however, adopted a line that was wholly inexcusable. He sought an interview with Mr. Baron Parke—who, it must be remembered, although not the presiding judge,

was assisting at the trial—communicated to him
the confession of his client, and asked his advice.
This conduct placed the judge in a most painful
position, and was grievously unjust to the accused.
It is probable that if Baron Parke had not been
taken by surprise, he would have declined to
express any opinion. I happen, however, to know
that, having learnt that the prisoner did not intend
to relieve his counsel from the defence, the learned
baron said that of course he must go on with it.
And, if he gave any advice at all, this was the only
advice he could give, and ought to have been
patent to the inquirer ; and certainly no censure
can be too severe upon the conduct of Phillipps,
who, when assailed for his management of the
case, violated the confidence that his interview
with Baron Parke demanded, and endeavoured to
excuse himself by saying he had acted under that
learned judge's advice.

I heard Phillipps's speech : it was extremely
eloquent. He made the most of some indiscre-
tions in his opponent's opening, but he was over-
weighted by the facts ; and certainly, since I have
been at the bar juries have not shown themselves
apt to be carried away by flowers of rhetoric.
Many of those used by him in this speech were not
only in bad taste, whatever might have been the
circumstances, but upon this occasion they were

utterly unjustifiable. I have refreshed my memory
of some of them, from a most useful and admirably-
arranged work of a Mr. Irving, called 'Annals
of our Time,' and from his work I extract the following specimens : ' Supposing him to be guilty
of the murder, which is known to Almighty God
alone'; 'I hope for the sake of his eternal soul that
he is innocent.' Such expressions from the mouth
of an advocate possessing the knowledge that
Phillipps did at the time he used them, were not
only offensive to good taste, but scarcely escaped
conveying a positive falsehood.

It is of the essence of advocacy that counsel
should under no circumstances convey his own
belief, or use expressions calculated to do so ; and
the only excuse that I can find for Phillipps is from
the knowledge that he always composed his important speeches before he delivered them, and
that up to the morning of the last day he believed
that Courvoisier was innocent. But whilst this may
redeem him from the imputation of conveying a
falsehood, it does not excuse the language in which
he indulged.

There is not, I think, any ground for saying
that he endeavoured to fix guilt, by unworthy
means, upon a servant girl. It may be said that
in every case where it is acknowledged that an
offence has been committed the defence of the

client must be founded upon the assumption that
some one else is guilty; but, excepting those expressions to which I have alluded, and which do not
point to any one in particular, I cannot recall anything that went beyond the bounds of legitimate
advocacy ; and I am sure that, whatever his faults
of taste and judgment, he would not have been
capable of so grave a crime.

He felt very bitterly the comments made upon
him by the press. I think they went beyond what
his conduct deserved, but, as I have been obliged
to admit, he certainly laid himself open to very
grave censure. I suppose few counsel have defended
more accused persons than myself, and I must allow
that innocence was not the characteristic feature
of the majority of my clients ; but I cannot remember any case in which I received an unqualified
admission of guilt. The utmost that approached
to it was a mild suggestion that if the evidence was
too strong for me to obtain an acquittal, it was
hoped that I would save my client from transportation.

I think that it may not be unserviceable at the
existing time to make a few observations upon this
subject. I am greatly struck by many of the features that now present themselves in connection
with crime. I think they are very formidable, more
so than ever I remember them, and, nuless they are

checked, point to an appalling future. There seems to me to be more abstract brutality amongst the criminal classes, and more recklessness of human life, and certainly the contingencies to whiôh the police are subjected whilst executing their functions are extremely frightful. The question, therefore, must come to the front, whether our present punishments are the most efficacious that can be applied.

When transportation was in force it created much dread to the criminals. There was a mystery attendant upon it, and a sense of final separation from every home tie. It operated also most strongly upon their friends and accomplices, thus creating, what is most to be desired, an efficient example to others. Now their friends know where they are, and in the miserable holes in which they themselves grovel, in cold, starvation, and wretchedness, they are apt almost to envy the food and warmth of a prison. There is also another point to be considered, if I am right in the view that I have formed. There are classes of criminals that can never be reformed whilst they are allowed to remain in this country, and yet their offences may not justify imprisonment for life. Practically a gaol educates them for graver ones. These include thieves from their birth, but who carry on their trade without resorting to violence. In another country they might find an

opening for redemption; in this, none. There may
be political grounds which make it impossible to
revert to the system of transportation. With these
I am not capable of dealing; but my experience
may be trusted for knowing that, next to death, it
inflicted the greatest terror, and to those capable
and desirous of repentance the only chance of re-
formation.

The crimes, however, that are now creating a
feeling allied to terror in the public mind are those
which subject our fellow-creatures to death or
cruel injury, and the question requires very grave
consideration and a freedom from morbid sentiment-
ality. The punishment of death is still continued,
and is thought to be sufficient to intimidate brutal
offenders; and of one thing I have no doubt, that
there is no example of a criminal, under a capital
sentence, who would not with joy exchange the
penalty for any other form of punishment known to
our law. Why, if it be inflicted and is supposed to
be thus efficacious in any case, should it be applied
to a result and not to the intention? Why should
a villain, armed with a revolver, maim a man for life
whilst in the performance of his duty and escape the
gallows? I think that the police ought to be told
that they shall be furnished at least with every pro-
tection possible. There were many conscientious
and kindly-hearted people who objected to the lash

being used; but surely if a deliberate war is waged by crime, and carried on by reckless violence and brutality against society, the most efficacious means ought to be used to defeat it. I am quite aware that any punishment that shocks the bulk of thinking and observant people could not be established; but humanitarianism may be carried too far, and we have arrived at a crisis when order must assert itself in language which will produce a deterrent effect upon criminals.

Whilst upon the subject of scoundrels and their doings, it will not be amiss to mention two who, amongst a crowd of smaller ones, flourished about the time of the Courvoisier trial. The cut-throats and garotters who at different periods have infested the metropolis were not greater pests than the proprietors of two newspapers called the ' Age ' and the ' Satirist.' The weapons with which they effected their robberies were slander and threats. They hunted out the secrets of families, and lived upon the fears of those to whom they appertained, and for some time these miscreants drove a thriving trade. Their names were, I believe, Westmacott and Barnard Gregory. I witnessed the former in the dress circle of Covent Garden Theatre howling under the horsewhip of Mr. Charles Kemble, whose daughter he had foully slandered, and I

had the satisfaction of convicting the latter at the
Old Bailey.

A volume might be filled with a record of their
villanies, and of the desolation that followed upon
their trail.   Let us hope that, like the murders
committed by professional duellists, they are the
filthy emanations of a bygone age, and are buried
in the infamy generated by their existence.

CHAPTER VIII.

THE CENTRAL COURT.

WILLIAM CLARKSON enjoyed a large business at the Central Court. He was not without ability of a certain kind, which was greatly assisted by his connection by marriage with a respectable firm of solicitors. Loud-voiced and swaggering, with one undeviating form of cross-examination, whatever might be the position or character of the witness, and that the very reverse of gentle or refined, he did much to maintain the opprobrium attaching to those who practised at the court. He was by no means considerate to his juniors, but succumbed at once to those capable of resistance. My recollection does not furnish me with any circumstances in his career, professionally or privately, that I can record to his advantage.

William Henry Bodkin was a man of a different type, and, in my opinion, if his education had been equal to his natural ability he would have attained a very high position. He was acute and clear-headed, and, as I have already mentioned, he was very successful in the civil business of the Middlesex

Sessions. He was a pleasant companion and extremely popular, and there were many, including myself, who received from him substantial marks of kindness.

When Mr. Phillipps obtained the appointment which I have recorded in the last chapter, I acquired a considerable accession of business, which, however, greatly diminished upon the advent of Mr. Charles Wilkins, a man who had already attained a high position at sessions in the North of England. He was at once patronised by the solicitors practising in the court, and the qualities he possessed were calculated to create early impressions in his favour. An imposing person and a deep sonorous voice controlled the audience. He was a fluent speaker, and arranged the matter he had to deal with very clearly. His experiences in many walks of life [1] must have furnished him with extensive knowledge of human nature ; his mind, however, was incapable of grasping the niceties of law, and he possessed no readiness in dealing with any matter suddenly started. A successful repartee threw him upon his back, and ridicule drove him frantic. He greatly diminished my business when first he came, but I fancy after a time I discovered his weak points,

[1] There were many stories told of the vicissitudes of his life which I have no means of verifying. He was at one time certainly in the medical profession, and at another an actor in the provinces.

and I do not think he maintained the reputation he had gained when he first joined the sessions. He afterwards changed the scene of his labours by taking the coif, and in a certain class of civil business again, for a certain time, obtained considerable success. Whilst practising at the Central Court he defended a solicitor, named Barber, in a very celebrated trial, of which I propose hereafter to give some account.

Subsequently to his departure I shared the lead with Mr. Parry, a man of great knowledge, power, and ability, until both of us quitted the field and followed Mr. Wilkins's example by taking the degree of the coif. We were often subsequently brought in special to the Central Court, and probably even upon this stage did not lose much by our promotion.

Before concluding my recollections of the Court I ought to mention two firms of solicitors who divided between them much of the defence business. Mr. Harmer, an alderman of the City of London, was at the head of one of them, and carried on business in Hatton Garden. His appearance indicated good living and good nature; he was gifted with great shrewdness, and possessed, amongst the classes whose natural destination was the Old Bailey, an immense reputation, and a most profound confidence was reposed

in him by a large body of clients, none of whom
had reason to regret their trust. He was rejected
as Lord Mayor upon the ground of certain opinions,
now to be found in many respectable journals, that
were ventilated in the 'Dispatch' newspaper, of
which he was proprietor. He realised a good
fortune, and built a villa on the banks of the
Thames, which he christened Ingress Abbey, but
which his friends called Newgate, where he entertained with great hospitality.

The other firm to which I allude was that of
Messrs. Lewis and Lewis of Ely Place, the senior
partner of whom, of small stature and quiet manner, with features characteristic of shrewdness and
a kindly nature, might often have been seen unpre-
tendingly making his way to the barristers' table.
His movements were watched with anxiety and
hope as he quietly walked about and slipped a
brief into the hands of a pleased recipient. His
firm possessed a large business, which he principally had built up by means in all respects honourable to himself. There were two other solicitors
of high standing and character who did a large
business, Mr. Humphreys and Mr. Wontner, but
they more usually appeared on the part of the
prosecutions.

What was called the Rope-walk was represented
by a set of agents clean neither in character nor

person, and I fear that the guinea eagerly sought by counsel in his early days told a sad tale of misery and self-denial endured by those who, as too often is the case, had to suffer for the sins of their relatives.

During my experience I have rarely known a thoroughly innocent person convicted, although there are certain charges scarcely sustained by strict evidence, but which carry with them a moral conclusion, and in which juries are apt to reject law and yield to prejudice ; but little evil arises from such results, and substantial justice is obtained.

I must, however, except one class of cases in which I have seen very grave errors committed by juries, and I fear that many innocent people have suffered. I allude to charges preferred by women against the opposite sex. Juries in many of these instances seem to bid adieu to common sense. The tears of a good-looking girl efface arguments of counsel and the suggestions of reason. However absurd and incredible the story told may be, a fainting fit at an appropriate time removes from their minds all its improbabilities. I have often wished that such charges might be disposed of by a jury of matrons. In cases that might fairly be the subject of an action before a civil tribunal the juries take up a high moral tone, and think themselves justified in inflicting the punishment awarded to one of the highest of crimes. I could record many instances in which, I believe, there has been a lamentably wrong conclusion arrived at against the person charged. In one case that I was engaged in, and in which the jury would scarcely listen to me, they were persuaded by the earnest exhortations of the judge to acquit the prisoner, but they appended to their finding the hope that his lordship would see that he was severely punished.

I remember a fashionable perruquier being tried many years ago at the Central Court for an outrage upon a young person in his employment. I cannot give the details of the story, which carried to my mind falsehood upon the face of it, but being plausibly told by a weeping complainant of prepossessing appearance, the hearts of the jury were moved, and their common sense was washed out. He was convicted and sentenced to a long term of transportation, which was, however, subsequently remitted.

A good story, for the truth of which I should, however, be sorry to vouch, is told, that the wife of the Governor of New South Wales, happening to be in England, implored the Home Secretary to carry out the sentence, as there was not a decent hairdresser in the colony.

It is well known that the Old Bailey, rechristened the Central Criminal Court when its jurisdiction was enlarged, was of civic origin, and still retains its original character. The aldermen, although they act by deputy, are judges, the Lord Mayor being the nominal head. The sheriffs represented by the under-sheriffs appertain to it; and these latter perform their more painful functions through the medium of the executioner. The citizens of London and their representatives have, in the days when the liberties of the people were threatened, made many a gallant stand, and done good service, and for this deserve the gratitude of posterity; but now the Lord Mayor, his state coach, the aldermen, the men in armour, the sword-bearer, and the City marshal are tawdry and useless monuments of a past age. The magisterial functions are discharged by paid clerks, of whom the aldermen are merely the mouthpieces, and might just as well be represented by their chains and robes. The mode by which officers called upon to perform high judicial duties are elected is a scandal to the age. The great merchants shrink from all connection with the corporation; and the definition of a good chief magistrate is one who has been most profuse in his hospitalities.

I should be very ungrateful if, in recording my opinion of the aldermen in their public capacity, I were not to acknowledge the number of most estimable, kindly, and excellent men who have at all times belonged to their body, and, during the early period of my practice at the Central Court, I and other members of the bar had to thank them for very liberal and unpretentious hospitality.. My comments apply solely to their position in relation to the administration of justice, which I regard as mischievous and absurd.

There was one alderman of whom I have a very distinct recollection: this was Sir Peter Laurie. He was a great friend of my father: he was a shrewd and far-seeing Scotchman, quaint and conceited, but with plenty of sound good sense and an honourable character. I mention him, however, not so much on his own account as to introduce to my readers one of the most original rogues of the time, and the mode in which, upon one occasion, Sir Peter dealt with him. Joseph Adie was his name, and amongst other modes of raising money he hit upon one of circulating letters to numerous people, professing that he had obtained knowledge which would be most beneficial to them, and by these means for a time he drove a thriving trade.

He was brought up before Sir Peter, who, finding that he had committed no punishable offence, was obliged to discharge him; but in doing so the worthy alderman said, by way of reprimand: 'Now,

Joseph, if any one wants to know your character refer him to me.' Adie, in all his future letters, headed them ' referred, by permission, to Sir Peter Laurie.' Ultimately Mr. Adie fell a victim to a suit by the post-office authorities for the price of stamps he had omitted to pay, and in default was sent to gaol. Whether he has since flowered in some other shape I know not; if so, probably he has also thought it convenient to appear in some other name.

As a wayfarer passed in the neigbourhood of the Mansion House about the period I have been more particularly recording, he might frequently have seen two neatly dressed personages, somewhat past middle age. They bore a great likeness to one another, although one affected juvenility in a brown wig, the other wearing his own perfectly white hair. Each presented a rosy-faced countenance, and a mild benevolence appeared to beam upon it; they might have been the brothers Cheeryble. They were the brothers Forester, the celebrated City officers; their hands were never profaned by touching vulgar thieves, and those whom they did touch usually terminated a career of great crime upon the gallows.

Notwithstanding their occupations, they were really as kindly as they looked. In many a heart-rending scene they had, as far as their duty would allow them, given solace to the afflicted. And their

evidence in court was always truthful and unex-
aggerated. I have had many a gossip with both
of them, and heard some painful episodes of criminal life.

The institution of the new police probably
superseded their employment. Their cheery faces
are no more seen, probably no longer exist. I
have no doubt, if living, they are provided for by
the generosity of the corporation, never wanting
towards those who have served them conscien-
tiously.

It is only right, whilst mentioning the celebrities
connected with the Old Bailey, that I should allude
to one other personage. Rarely met with upon
festive occasions, he was, nevertheless, accustomed
to present himself after dinner on the last day of
the sessions. He was a decently dressed, quiet-
looking man. Upon his appearance he was presented with a glass of wine. This he drank to
the health of his patrons, and expressed with
becoming modesty his gratitude for past favours,
and his hopes for favours to come. He was Mr.
Calcraft, the hangman.[1]

[1] This occurred in a past generation.

CHAPTER IX.

FRIENDS.

AMONGST the friendships I formed and greatly valued
during the early period of my career at the bar
was that of Charles Edward Jerningham, nephew,
I believe, of the Earl of Stafford. We sat together
briefless at the Central Court; we shared a room
over a butcher's shop during the assizes at Maidstone; and sighed in unison for the trumpets that
announced the dinner hour to be approaching. He
was a charming companion and an accomplished
scholar. In consequence of his health failing he
quitted the profession and went abroad, and I never
saw him again, although I occasionally heard from
him. I have, however, had the pleasure of meeting
his son, Hubert, a gentleman who has distinguished
himself in diplomacy and literature.[1] Huddleston
and Jerningham were in those days my most intimate companions at the bar.

I was, however, fortunate in possessing some
very pleasant acquaintances out of the profession,
and amongst them was a gentleman well known in
London society—Mr. Dubois. He lived in Sloane

[1] He has now added M.P. to his distinctions.

Street, where he exercised a liberal and ungrudg-
ing hospitality to a large circle of friends, chiefly
connected with literature and art.   Amongst them
were the brothers Smith, authors of the ' Rejected
Addresses,' of whom, however, I have no very
precise recollection; and Barham, the charming
author of that wonderful collection of drolleries,
' The Ingoldsby Legends.'   This gentleman I also
had the pleasure of meeting elsewhere, and his
quiet, refined humour has often been a source of
great delight to me.   Theodore Hook—bright, im-
provident, reckless genius—was a constant visitor,
and with him a little rosy-faced individual, his tried
friend and worshipper, Mr. Hill.   This latter was
a mystery.   No one knew when he came into the
world, and it used to be said that if really he had
been born after a legitimate fashion, the records of
his birth had been lost in the fire of London.   Mr.
Dubois, in addition to being a recognised patron of
literature, performed judicial functions in a small
debts court, in a street leading out of Holborn,
called the Court of Requests, but his duties never
seemed to give him anxiety or to affect his cordial
good temper.   His house formed a fair example of
the hospitality of a former generation.   The dinner
hour, as far as I remember, was half-past five, when
the guests met substantial fare and a hearty welcome, the pleasure derived from which was greatly

enhanced by the cordiality and kindness of Mrs. Dubois and her pretty and accomplished daughter. But the hour when fun reigned supreme approached nearer to midnight. Then it was that I have heard Theodore Hook, who seemed to brighten for the occasion, sing some of his most amusing songs. They were supposed to be extemporary, but his friend Hill might be detected furnishing a cue.

Poor Theodore, although upon these occasions brilliant, was a sad wreck when seen at other times. He had lived hard, which meant something in those days, and had seriously damaged his constitution. As is well known, he once filled the post of Treasurer of the Colony of the Mauritius, and his carelessness had resulted in a serious deficiency in the funds over which he had control, no imputation, however, beyond carelessness resting upon his character. His answer when asked how he came to leave the island has been often told. ' It was,' he said, ' through a complaint of the chest.' He was sued by the Government for the amount deficient, and thrown into the Queen's Bench prison ; a step which would not have been taken but that they were forced into it by the Opposition, who were furious at the attacks made upon Queen Caroline in the ' John Bull ' newspaper, which he edited. My friend Dubois as Duberly, and Hill as Hull, will be recognised in his amusing novel of ' Gilbert

Gurney;' and I am inclined to think that the description in that work of the scene at the Old Bailey and of the deaf judge will fully bear comparison with the great trial of 'Bardell *v*. Pickwick,' immortalised by Dickens.

I also remember Poole, the author of 'Paul Pry,' a character suggested to him, umbrella and all, by Mr. Hill. It used to be the pride of this latter gentleman to learn everything about his neighbours. He could inform his associates which of their friends had a party, and what they had for dinner. He used to look down the areas and watch the confectioner's man; in fact, he acted the *rôle* of a busybody for the amusement of his friends, but was too much liked ever to have been a mischievous one.

It was about the time of these convivial meetings that I became a member of the Clarence Club, called by its detractors the Clearance, from the fact of its having been founded upon the Literary Union, dissolved to get rid of some objectionable members. There were many agreeable people belonging to it. Amongst others, a prominent member was Mr. Dilke, founder of the 'Athenæum' journal, father of the first baronet, who also was a member, and grandfather of the present statesman. Those who knew this gentleman well spoke of him as possessing an intellect of great capacity and

power. His son, an old friend of mine, was a very
agreeable companion. He was most useful in the
management of the very difficult details connected
with the Exhibition of 1851, and his services were
much appreciated by the late Prince Consort, himself no mean judge of the capacity of those with
whom he had dealings, and in recognition of them a
baronetcy was conferred upon him by her Majesty.

Tom Campbell, the author of ' The Pleasures of
Memory,' did not present a romantic figure ; and
his carelessness about dress rendered his appearance much less agreeable than his poetry. The
late Lord Justice James was also a member. I was
not personally acquainted with him. I fancy that
he always exhibited those marks of ability which,
when he was promoted to the Bench, rendered
him one of its greatest ornaments.

Another gentleman, a member of the club, and
with whom I had the pleasure of being on terms
of intimacy, was the late Frank Stone, an artist
who possessed a great charm. There are few pictures, to my thinking, more pleasant to look at than
those that came from his brush. His health was
not good, and he died whilst in the full vigour of
his mind. I need not mention how honourably
and successfully his son Marcus Stone has followed
in his father's steps.

As I am professing to write experiences of my

VOL. I.   I

own life, I cannot forbear mentioning two members of the club who were intimate associates and
friends of mine. Their names are not inscribed upon
the tablets of fame, but they are worthy to be remembered. Captain Barberie was one of them, an
Englishman by parentage, but, being either born in
India or taken there very early, he presented a
complexion nearly Eastern. He had only one leg,
his other having been amputated at the thigh-
joint. He had served in India, and his limb was
shattered at one of the sieges which the British
had been obliged to raise, and it showed wonderful vitality, that, with the wounded leg dangling to
his body, he bore the fearful trial of a retreat
before it could be amputated. His face had the
mark upon it of a fearful cut which he received
from a native whom he had discovered embezzling
stores ; it also bore the marks of a severe attack of
small-pox which he had suffered from in India. I
have not drawn a very inviting picture of his personal appearance ; he was, nevertheless, pleasant to
look upon, and much beloved by his many friends.
His daily companion and associate was a Major
Henderson, also an Indian officer, who was wounded
at the same siege. His wound was upon the head,
and had been received whilst storming the fortress
where his friend had his leg shattered. He was
taken up apparently dead, but it turned out that

the bullet had carried his handkerchief, which he wore under his regimental cap, into the wound, and with the handkerchief the bullet came out. He was trepanned, and although at times suffering great pain, lived for many years after.

One day Barberie was missing from the club; and when on the next day he did not turn up, I went to Duke Street where he lived, and, opening the door of his chambers, saw him stretched upon a sofa. 'Do not come in,' he said to me. 'I have got the small-pox.' Of course I asked whether I could assist him. He said that Henderson was doing all that he required. Daily inquiries were made after him by his friends, and, to the satisfaction of all, we heard that the crisis was past, and he was in a sound, healthy sleep. Ten minutes after, he was dead. A tray of crockery had been dropped in the court-yard and startled him from his sleep. His mind wandered for a moment, and then passed into eternity.

Although naturally very clever, he was a perfect child in the world's ways, and a designing woman having obtained great influence over him, his friends feared he would marry her. He was not upon good terms with his relatives, and had made a will bequeathing everything to her. One afternoon, shortly before his death, Henderson, myself, and he were at the club, and we were laughing at him for his infatuation; he got very much annoyed, left the club, and, as we heard afterwards, went off to the dwelling of this person, and, being quite unexpected at that hour, he found her in company which fully justified our opinions. He came home, destroyed the will, and never left the house afterwards. His illness prevented his making another disposition of his property, and his relatives got all he left behind him. He received a pension of 50l. per annum for the loss of his leg, and he had an amusing mode of appraising everything according to that value. He would describe, for example, a sum of 25l. as half a leg, and in this way divided it into fractions with great accuracy.

Barberie wrote a very vivid account of his calamity in 'Bentley's Miscellany,' headed 'How I Lost my Leg.' He was only thirty-five years old when he died, after undergoing more misfortunes than most people are subject to in the longest life, and succumbed at last to the combined action of a disease he had previously suffered from and the carelessness of a stupid servant. Major Henderson survived his friend for some years; but the affairs of the club not having been prosperous it was dissolved, the members were scattered, and amongst others I lost sight of this gentleman.

I had the pleasure of the acquaintance of Mr. Bransby Cooper, the nephew of the eminent surgeon, Sir Astley Cooper. He was himself in the same profession; but early in his career had the misfortune to fail in an operation, which cost the patient his life.

His mode of performing it was severely criticised by Mr. Wakley in the ' Lancet,' and, although he obtained a verdict in an action he brought against that gentleman, the damages were scarcely sufficient to clear him from blame. In another respect, through no fault of his own, he was unfortunate. His uncle retired from the profession, leaving him in the occupation of his house in Spring Gardens, and securing for him one prosperous year; but, getting sick of leisure, Sir Astley returned suddenly from abroad, and, as I have heard the story, wandered to the end of the Chain Pier at Brighton, having half a mind to terminate the misery of idleness. Instead, however, of availing himself of the ocean for that purpose, he ordered a post-chaise, and turned up in Spring Gardens as quickly as four horses could carry him, and there renewed his profession, which he carried on successfully for many years. Bransby Cooper, after this, although possessing surgical skill and excellent judgment, never obtained any hold upon the public. He used often to complain to me of a soreness and irritation in his throat, which he attributed to a laceration caused by his having swallowed a fish-

bone. He died suddenly whilst at the Athenæum
Club, his death being caused by a cancer in the
throat. It is probable that he was aware of the
fact, although he affected to ignore it.

Wakley was a man of mark in his time, and the
action brought against him by Bransby Cooper
gave him notoriety. He was himself plaintiff
against the County Fire Office to recover the
amount insured upon his house, which had been
burnt down, and the office raised the defence that
he had himself done it. He recovered a verdict;
but I believe the damages were never paid, and he
took no steps to enforce them.

He was a popular speaker, and was returned to
Parliament for a metropolitan borough. Some one,
alluding to a speech he had made, remarked to
Sheil, the Irish orator, ' that he would never set
the Thames on fire.' ' No,' said Sheil, ' unless he
had first insured it.' He became coroner for
Middlesex, and in that capacity held an inquest upon
a body presumably that of Mr. John Sadleir, member
for Sligo, an Under Lord of the Treasury, and the
perpetrator of stupendous frauds. The corpse was
found upon Hampstead Heath, and it was alleged
that death had resulted from suicide. There were
circumstances about the appearance and the finding that led some people to doubt whether it really
was the body of Sadleir; but Mr. Wakley knew
him well, and could make no mistake, and it was

also identified by Mr. Edwin James, the Queen's Counsel; but, as far as I remember, these were the only witnesses to its identity.

Bransby Cooper was fond of narrating an anecdote of his uncle in connection with a murder committed at Rotherhithe by a man named Patch. The deceased had been shot; and from the position that he was in at the time, and the direction of the wound, Sir Astley, then Mr., Cooper was satisfied that the shot was fired by a left-handed man.

Patch assured his counsel that such was not the case with him; but, when called upon to plead, held up his left hand. It may be necessary to mention, for the information of some of my readers, that at that period the prisoner pleading was always told to hold up his hand. He was convicted and executed.

I may here mention another acquaintance that I formed, of not so reputable a character as those whom I have had the pleasure of describing heretofore. This was an Italian nobleman, who came over to this country with good introductions, and whose manners and varied information were calculated to create a very favourable impression upon society. It turned out that, although his rank was unquestionable, he was one of a gang of forgers, and engaged in carrying out a conspiracy of a very remarkable and daring character. The course contemplated was to pass simultaneously, in the principal cities upon the Continent, forged letters of credit purporting to issue from Messrs. Glyn and other bankers in London. The scheme failed by a mere accident ; and the circumstances connected with it were investigated and exposed with great ability by the ' Times ' newspaper, against which journal, in consequence of its strictures, a person who was supposed to be an accomplice brought an action. It was tried at the Croydon summer assizes in the year 1841, and the substantial correctness of the articles was clearly established. The merchants of London subscribed for a testimonial to the paper to mark their sense of the great ability which, regardless of expense, had been exhibited by it in exposing the fraud. The proprietors dedicated the large sum of money subscribed to public purposes.

It was said that the nobleman committed suicide, but no very authentic account of the circumstance, if it really occurred, ever reached this country. I cannot help thinking that I had some hand in assisting the design of the conspirators, as I was inveigled to a party at the Grecian Tavern in the Strand, where I lost what was for me a considerable sum of money to the nobleman. I learnt afterwards the character of the people whom I met, all of whom were gentlemen by birth and swindlers by profession.

CHAPTER X.

SUIT IN THE HOUSE OF LORDS.

IT is somewhat remarkable that the first case of much importance in which I was engaged was in the House of Lords, before a tribunal composed of the following noblemen: the Earl of Devon, chairman; Lord Lyndhurst, Lord Campbell, the Earl of Radnor, the Earl of Lonsdale, Lord Sudeley, Lord Mountford, and others. A bill had been introduced to annul the marriage of a young lady, Miss Esther Field, contracted with a person named Samuel Brown, upon the grounds of coercion and fraud on his part, accompanied by the allegation that the marriage had not been consummated. The circumstances were very extraordinary. The lady was possessed of a large fortune—£1,200 per annum in land, and £40,000 in money. She was barely eighteen years old, whilst Brown was fifty-two, of humble origin, and no apparent means. However, he prevailed upon the lady to marry him, much, I fancy, to the disgust of a young gentleman, the son of an attorney, who would very willingly have taken his place, and probably, in the event of the bill having passed, would have succeeded in doing so. There was a formidable array of counsel in support of it —Sir Fitzroy Kelly, Mr. Rolt, Sir John Bayley, Mr. Walford, and Mr. Austin. I was alone in opposition to the bill.

Sir F. Kelly opened the case with a considerable amount of colouring, which was maintained by Esther under the examination of Mr. Rolt. In my cross-examination I endeavoured to make her relate the facts in a natural manner, and to get rid of the exaggerations that had coloured her evidence in chief. Other witnesses were called, and Mr. Rolt having addressed the House in favour of the bill, the case was adjourned until the following Friday. On that day I was about to address their lordships, when the Earl of Devon interposed, and I copy from the 'Times' of August 11, 1848, the observations that he made :—

'He said that their lordships did not feel it necessary to call upon the learned counsel to address them. He had in the first instance, he was free to admit, come down to the House with a strong bias in favour of the bill for annulling the marriage ; but the evidence he had heard, and the able cross-examination of the learned counsel against the bill, had created a contrary opinion in his mind. In that opinion he was supported not only by Lord Brougham, whom, in common with other learned lords, members of this House, he had consulted, but by Lord Lyndhurst, who had most carefully perused the whole of the proceedings in the Court of Chancery, and had heard the arguments and evidence which had been offered at the bar of their lordships' House, and informed him that there was not a sufficient case to sustain a bill for annulling the marriage of this young lady. From the Lord Chancellor he had also received a similar intimation.

' Such being not only his own opinion, but that of his noble and learned friends, he felt it impossible for him to move the further progress of the bill.'

The eminent physician, Dr. Locock, had been subpœnaed as a witness by the petitioner, but was not called.

At the end of the first day, Lord Lyndhurst came up to the bar of the House, where I was standing, mentioned that he had known my father, and paid me a kind compliment upon the mode in which I had conducted the case, concluding by asking me whether I intended to call witnesses; and upon my replying that it depended upon the result of a consultation, remarked, with a significant smile, ' I do not think you will.'

It will not be out of place here to make some remarks upon cross-examination. The records of courts of justice from all time show that truth cannot in a great number of cases tried be reasonably expected. Even when witnesses are honest, and have no intention to deceive, there is a natural tendency to exaggerate the facts favourable to the cause for which they are appearing, and to ignore the opposite circumstances : and the only means known to English law by which testimony can be sifted is cross-examination. By this agent, if skilfully used, falsehood ought to be exposed, and exaggerated statements reduced to their true dimensions. An unskilful use of it, on the contrary, has a tendency to uphold rather than destroy. If the principles upon which cross-examination ought to be founded are not understood and acted upon, it is worse than useless, and it becomes an instrument against its employer. The reckless asking of a number of questions on the chance of getting at something is too often a plan adopted by unskilful advocates, and noise is mistaken for energy. Mr. Baron Alderson once remarked to a counsel of this type, ' Mr. ——, you seem to think that the art of cross-examination is to examine crossly.'

In order to attain success in this branch of advocacy, it is necessary for counsel to form in his own mind an opinion upon the facts of the case, and the character and probable motives of a witness, before asking a question. This, doubtless, requires experience; and the success of his cross-examination must depend upon the accuracy of the judgment he forms.

Great discernment is needful to distinguish material from unimportant discrepancies, and never to dwell long upon immaterial matters; but if a witness intends to commit perjury, it is rarely useful to press him upon the salient points of the case, with which he probably has made himself thoroughly acquainted, but to seek for circumstances for which he would not be likely to prepare himself.

And it ought, above all things, to be remembered by the advocate, that when he has succeeded in making a point, he should leave it alone until his turn comes to address the jury upon it. If a dishonest witness has inadvertently made an admission injurious to himself, and, by the counsel's dwelling upon it, becomes aware of the effect, he will endeavour to shuffle out of it and perhaps succeed in doing so.

The object of cross-examination is not to produce startling effects, but to elicit facts which will support the theory intended to be put forward. Sir William Follett asked the fewest questions of any counsel I ever knew; and I have heard many cross-examinations from others listened to with rapture by an admiring client, each question of which has been destruction to his case.

What is called a severe cross-examination, when applied to a truthful witness, only makes the truth stand out more clearly; and unless counsel is able to arrive in his own mind at a satisfactory opinion, it is far better to ask nothing than to flounder on with the chance of getting out something by a crowd of questions. A truthful witness usually adheres to the dry statement of facts, and avoids diverting attention by introducing irrelevant matter; and I think a remark I made to a jury upon one occasion is a sound one, It was upon a trial before Chief Justice Erle. I had put a question to a witness as to what he was doing at a particular time, this being a matter important to the inquiry. 'I was talking to a lady,' was his answer; adding, 'I will tell you who she was, if you like. You know her very well.' I made no observation at the time, but when addressing the jury said that my experience led me to the conclusion that honest witnesses endeavoured to keep themselves to the facts they came to prove, but that lying ones endeavoured to distract the attention by introducing something irrelevant; and I think this remark is worth consideration, and points out one of the tests of truth or falsehood in a person under examination.

Some judges upon the bench never shone in this branch of advocacy, and scarcely appreciate the value of it, and a refinement that now attends trials, and contrasts in many respects favourably with the coarseness of a former period, occasionally interferes with the force and persistence required in dealing with some persons in the box.

In the equity courts, the notion of cross-examination is ludicrous; it has, however, the merit of being thoroughly inoffensive,

I have heard two or three specimens of it. In these cases the witnesses had filed affidavits which the adverse counsel examined from, and made them repeat orally what they had already sworn to, as if the object of the process was to obtain from the mouth of the witness in court what had already been put upon paper in the solicitor's office.

An experienced equity judge once said to me in relation to a question I had asked, 'Really, this is a long way from the point.' 'I am aware of that, my lord,' was my answer. 'If I were to begin any nearer, the witness would discover my object.'

It is impossible to over-estimate the acuteness and argumentative powers of the judges and practitioners in the equity courts, but I am confident that they would find great assistance if the examination of witnesses were less of a sham.

Embarrassment exhibited under a searching cross-examination is not to be relied on as a proof of falsehood; the novelty of the position or constitutional nervousness may frequently occasion it.

I remember a remarkable instance of this in a trial in which I was engaged to defend a prisoner. It was a curious case. Messrs. Coutts, the bankers, were in the habit at certain periods of remitting specie to a bank at Oxford by a coach that went to that city. The money was contained in a box, and placed under the charge of the coachman. Upon a particular day, when the supposed box arrived at its destination, it was found to contain rubbish, the real one having been subtracted. It was proved that my client, who was a passenger, had got down before the end of the journey, with no apparent excuse, and did not take his seat again. Beyond this, however, there was little to sustain the charge against him. The coachman naturally was a principal witness, but became so embarrassed, and answered questions in so shuffling a manner, although with perfect truth, that both judge and jury believed that he was an accomplice in the robbery, and in this opinion I confess I shared.

My client was acquitted, but shortly afterwards was tried and convicted of another offence. I took the opportunity (I think, through the medium of the chaplain) to ask how the Oxford robbery had been effected, and learnt that the coachman had, against orders, gone into a public-house to get a glass of ale, and it was during his absence that the prisoner contrived to convey the dummy to an accomplice in front, receiving from him the genuine box, with which he decamped.

I have myself succeeded, by cross-examination, in cases where claims were made for injuries received in railway accidents, in showing that the claimant had not even been present at the time of the occurrence; and I may mention that, in a case tried this very year before the Lord Chief Justice, I assisted in exposing a very gross fraud of this nature attempted by a medical man. No witnesses were called by the company, which I represented, and upon my cross-examination, supplemented by some very important questions by the judge, the jury, upon the plaintiff's evidence alone, found a verdict for the defendants, and I believe the plaintiff had not been near the place when the accident occurred.

Cross-examination has recently become more important than ever in sifting the evidence of professional witnesses in cases where injuries have been sustained from the above class of accidents, and in which the most eminent professional men occasionally fall into grave errors, and I feel obliged to add that some in the lower walks of the profession make the manufacture of these cases a not unprofitable trade. One of these worthies admitted in a recent trial that he might have been engaged in a hundred of them.

A remark was recently made by the Lord Chief Justice, which accords most thoroughly with my experience, that perjury is greatly on the increase, and although, when detected, severe punishments may help to check it, it must be remembered that cross-examination is the only means by which it can be exposed.

I cannot forbear relating an anecdote in connection with one of the most amiable and excellent of judges, the late Lord Hatherley, when he was Vice-Chancellor. I was counsel before him, and had to cross-examine a very plausible, but certainly not truthful, witness. I did so with some severity, and I imagine that I should have been successful before a jury.

His lordship, however, was of a different opinion, and was much struck with the ingenuousness of the young man, and he evidently thought that he had been exposed to a cruel ordeal. As the witness himself was going out of the court, he was heard to whisper to a friend, 'Why, the old gent believed every word I swore.' [1]

I was very well acquainted with Mr. Rolt, the second counsel in the case with an account of which I commenced this chapter. I visited at his house, and met him frequently at the Garrick Club, and at the houses of mutual friends. He was a most distinguished member of the Chancery bar, and became Lord Justice. He planted the seeds of a premature death by giving himself too

[1] The term applied to his lordship was not of so refined a description.

little relaxation from intensely hard work. I have seen him come into the club of an evening looking worn and exhausted, swallow a hasty dinner, and rush off to further labour. He earned a high reputation, but paid a heavy price for it. Very different in appearance and habits was another of the counsel, Sir John Bayley, son of the eminent Baron of the Exchequer. He was jovial and kindly, and, although esteemed a good lawyer, was more known for his social than his legal eminence; mainly through his support and assistance, I became a member of the Union Club, and through his kindness also I enjoyed some of the most charming of gatherings at the grounds of Mr. Lumley, situated on the bank of the Thames, near Hammersmith Bridge. He was at that time the lessee of Her Majesty's Theatre. The site of his villa is now occupied by wharves. There, in the midst of a most brilliant scene, were on these occasions assembled distinguished guests of different ranks, who were delighted to meet all that was bright and beautiful in the theatrical and operatic world. At one of these fêtes, I remember two ex-Chancellors enjoying the conversation of that most fascinating of danseuses, Mademoiselle Duvernay. No doubt, as Lord Campbell said of himself when he was met at Cremorne Gardens, they considered it their duty to study the habits of all classes of the community.

The period when this occurred renders it unnecessary for me to say that they were not Lord Selborne, Lord Cairns, or Lord Hatherley.

Mr. Delafield, who had been a member of the great brewing firm of Combe, Delafield, and Company, took to the less profitable venture of the Covent Garden Opera House, and he also gave charming parties of a similar character at a pretty villa on the Fulham side of Putney Bridge. The large fortune with which he retired from the brewery was soon engulfed in the expenses of his operatic venture ; and when, in after-years, I met him, as I did not unfrequently, he was living at Brussels for the sake of economy, but seemed to bear the loss of his fortune with philosophy and cheerfulness.

Sir Fitzroy Kelly and Mr. Austin were both men of mark, but I shall postpone any observations about them to a future chapter.

I trust that I shall not be thought guilty of unjustifiable vanity in recording the circumstances of the case commencing this chapter, and quoting the observations of Lord Devon. I hope also that in the comments that I have made upon the mode of dealing with witnesses it will not be considered that I arrogate to myself any superior knowledge. At the same time it is possible that the experience I have obtained in a long career may not be without its use to some of my younger professional friends.

CHAPTER XI.

FAMOUS AUTHORS.

UNDER the colonnade of Covent Garden there existed a cluster of taverns: Evans's, the Gordon, New and Old Hummums, the Tavistock, the Piazza, and the Bedford. The two last had been the resort of noblemen and people of rank and distinction in society, who dined there at hours that would now be considered early, and consumed a considerable quantity of port wine. So I have heard and read. When I knew the houses themselves their glory had waned, although the Piazza still carried its head somewhat higher than its neighbours. In a large room in this tavern was held a nightly meeting called the Shakespeare Club. Its name suggests its character, and that of the majority of its members. Here it was that for the first time I met Thackeray. His appearance has often been described, and, although he was then unknown to me, it at once commanded my attention—tall above the ordinary height and proportionately broad. His face had been disfigured by a blow received in boyhood, and in repose would have been called plain. Although characterised by great solidity, it was only when he lifted his eyes that it became illumined, and the observer felt that it was one of rare intelligence. When I met him upon this occasion I was not aware that he was the author of the papers published in 'Fraser's Magazine' entitled the Yellow Plush Correspondence, which, in its anonymous form, I had read with intense amusement, nor have I found reason upon reperusal to alter my judgment. I am not, however, a great worshipper of his more elaborate works, although I do not presume to dispute the great power, thought, and knowledge that they exhibit. They present an unpleasant, and I do not think entirely correct, view of human nature. I believe it is better than he paints it. Thackeray appears almost to divide it into knaves and fools. My experience—and much of it has been gained amongst what would be deemed the outcasts of society—is that in every class there is much that is good and estimable; but even assuming his views to be correct, and that his novels are skilful and accurate analyses of human nature, the scenes they exhibit sometimes pain, and do not always amuse, me. Colonel Newcome, the very pattern of amiability, presents an unpleasant picture whilst victimised by an Asiatic swindler, whom the reader sees through from the outset. Doubtless the Colonel's resignation in adversity is very noble, and affords an excellent example, but can hardly be called a pleasant picture.

I follow the career of Becky Sharpe with mingled compassion and disgust. I cannot imagine anything more repulsive than her betrayal of her husband. And I am not sure that the virtuous indignation of Colonel Crawley is quite consistent with his character as previously described. I do not forget ' Pendennis,' and the old Major—a perfect sketch ; and I am almost wonder-struck at the learning and research exhibited in ' Esmond ; ' but when I read a novel I want a hero who does not give me lessons, and I do not care for the anatomy of human nature, however skilfully it may be laid bare.

I am willing to admit and regret my heterodox opinions, and own myself to be whatever the great mass of Thackeray's admirers may choose to call me ; but they are my opinions, and I do not wish to make capital by borrowing those of other people.

Although not amongst his intimate friends, I met him frequently. We were members together of the Garrick Club, and I often saw him elsewhere.

I never thought him an agreeable companion. He was very egotistical, greedy of flattery, and sensitive of criticism to a ridiculous extent. He may have possessed great powers of conversation,

but did not exhibit them upon the occasions when
I had an opportunity of judging.

He did not hesitate to introduce his associates
and the members of his club into his novels, and
one of these latter, a curious compound of drollery
and simplicity, named Archdeckne,[1] figures in 'Pendennis' under the name of Foker; and on one
occasion I think that Albert Smith had great reason
to complain of his proceedings.

This gentleman and a poor fellow now dead,
Joe Robbins, had been associates and friends; the
latter, who originally had been in a lucrative business, quitted it for the stage and got into a very
sad plight. I know that Albert Smith had been
most considerate and kind to him, but had on
one occasion refused to join in some subscription
that had been set on foot on his behalf. Thackeray
circulated throughout the club a caricature, in
which the likenesses were unmistakable. Robbins
was represented wounded by thieves and being
assisted by some good Samaritan, also portrayed,
whilst Albert Smith, the Pharisee of the parable,
was passing scornfully upon the other side. There
was another member of the club who had injudi-
ciously published some remarks about him, for
which he pursued him with but little considera-

[1] I am told that this gentleman was by no means offended
by the celebrity he obtained through figuring in Thackeray's
novel.

tion or mercy. And I cannot forbear expressing my sorrow that a man so really great should have descended to most unworthy sneers at another equally great man and brother author, Sir Edward Lytton Bulwer, as he did on several occasions.

The last time I saw him was about three weeks before his death. He was sitting alone at a table at Evans's, poring over an obscure Irish journal in which some derogatory remarks about himself were published. He attributed them to an individual whom I need not name, and was intensely angry, which I confess I thought at the time was eminently absurd. His description, however, of the Irish in many of his works was not calculated to make him popular in that country. Having ventured to make these strictures, founded upon my observation and judgment, of a man who has established a great mark on the literature of his age, I ought to mention a fact which was within my knowledge, that he suffered from a most painful and irritating disease, and also that among those who knew him well, and to whom he extended his confidence and friendship, he was most enthusiastically beloved.

I remember one other member of the Shakespeare Club, John Forster, the biographer of Dickens. His temper was not a very comfortable one to deal with, and I fancy was mainly instrumental in breaking the club up.

At the house of some very agreeable people named Levien, living in Woburn Place, I first had the pleasure of meeting Charles Dickens, and also his sister, a young lady of great talent and accomplishments, who unfortunately died when still quite young. Dickens had already won his spurs under the sobriquet of Boz. He and Thackeray happened to be contemporaries, otherwise there was no similarity between them either in their writings or their character.

The works of both of them, published as they were periodically, were eagerly looked forward to. Their styles were very different; it may be said that Thackeray invited thought and reflection, whilst Dickens, although by no means losing sight of the true delineation of human nature, showed that his main object was to amuse. How great a genius it must have been that immortalised Pickwick.

What other man could have enshrined such a mass of absurdities in the minds of the public by genuine fun and shrewd knowledge of human nature? Bardell against Pickwick is a burlesque, and yet there is nothing impossible in a deaf judge or an inflated address by counsel, and a speculative firm of attorneys may be found even during the present days of purity. My dear old friend Toole still creates roars of laughter whilst personating Serjeant Buzfuz, in a wig and gown with which I

presented him for the purpose. Mr. Pickwick
becomes almost a hero when he goes to prison upon
principle. Many of Dickens's novels had higher
ends, which they have fully attained, and some of
the characters are drawn with a force of description and knowledge certainly not surpassed by any
writer of any age.

Imagine yourself in the parlour of a country inn
on a wet day. How the misery you are looking
forward to is changed into content by the discovery
of one of his novels! They amuse man, woman,
and child alike, and they furnish good thoughts
and kindly feelings towards their fellow-creatures.
I was very much attached to Charles Dickens;
there was a brightness and geniality about him
that greatly fascinated his companions. His laugh
was so cheery, and he seemed so thoroughly to enter
into the feelings of those around him. He told a
story well and never prosily; he was a capital
listener, and in conversation was not in the slightest degree dictatorial.

He, like Thackeray, was very sensitive, and I
remember a period when his conduct had been so
misinterpreted that he suffered agonies. No man
possessed more sincere friends, or deserved them
better. He was the best after-dinner speaker I ever
heard, and I cannot forbear recording a trifling
incident that occurred the last time I met him,

and shortly before his death. We were both dining
at Mr. Cartwright's, in Old Burlington Street ; I
was sitting nearly opposite to him, and referred to
a speech that he had made at the previous Royal
Academy dinner in terms of praise certainly not
exaggerated. He replied, 'Praise from Sir Hubert!'
I and Mr. Spicer, a friend of his and mine, had
put him up at the Union Club, and, to our great
grief, the news of his death reached us upon the
day on which he would have been elected.

A mutual friend, and one equally dear to us
both, was Mr. Serjeant, afterwards Mr. Justice,
Talfourd, lawyer, orator, and poet. Those who
knew him will never forget his kindly, genial face,
the happiness radiating from it when imparting
pleasure to others, and his generous hospitality,
extended in no niggard spirit.

He occupied a large house in Russell Square,
and the gatherings that frequently took place in
it included not only those who had obtained
eminence in their profession, but the young who
were striving to do so. Science and literature were
represented by their most distinguished members.
Painters, poets, historians, and actors mingled
together and enjoyed themselves, Talfourd moving about and welcoming his miscellaneous company with cordial smiles and greeting. I remember poor Frank, his eldest son, and whose youth

showed much promise (terminated, unhappily, by premature death), bending over the chair of a pretty and popular actress with looks and words of devotion, and it will be no improper breach of confidence to say that she refused his hand lest at his early age she might injure his prospects. He was an amusing writer, and initiated the modern school of burlesque, and it is no reflection upon the clever authors of the present day to say that his works would bear comparison with any of them.

Macready, always the actor, was happy to be the guest of the author of 'Ion,' one of his best parts. And there also he could converse with Sir Edward Lytton Bulwer, whose plays of 'The Lady of Lyons' and 'Richelieu' had furnished him with brilliant materials for the display of his talents. The author of 'The Hunchback' was no unworthy or unconsidered guest. Huddleston also, who had been early appreciated by his host, who never lost the opportunity of giving beginners a lifting hand, was a frequent and favoured visitor.[1]

And Albert Smith, full of life and jollity, but who had not then climbed his mountain, seemed none the less happy because he had not yet obtained fame. How many others I might mention, and, alas! how many, with Talfourd himself, have left the earthly stage! I need not say that it was

[1] Mr. Huddleston went the same circuit as Mr. Serjeant Talfourd.

not only in social and literary life that Talfourd
distinguished himself. In the House of Commons
he was much respected, and his successful efforts in
carrying the Copyright Bill conferred a real boon
upon his brother authors. He attained one of the
objects of his ambition by a seat upon the bench,
and, as is well known, died suddenly whilst in the
performance of his duties at Stafford assizes.

In the slight sketch I have ventured to offer to
my readers I must not forget to mention the great
aid he received from the loving, true, and cordial
co-operation of Lady Talfourd, who, with her most
charming daughters and niece, assisted with heartfelt cordiality in diffusing happiness throughout
the assembly.

When at the bar, Mr. Serjeant Talfourd was
counsel, in conjunction with Campbell and Thesiger,
for Lord Melbourne in the action brought against
him by Mr. Norton for criminal conversation.
In his Diary, lately published, Lord Campbell
does not mention the names of either of these
gentlemen. Serjeant Talfourd was, as I know, retained at the express desire of Mrs. Norton, and
he always entertained an undoubting conviction of
her innocence. I was greatly interested in the
case, not only from its public character, but from
the fact of being acquainted with both Mr. and
Mrs. Norton, the former being a brother magis-

trate of my father. I had myself met the
lady upon one or two occasions. She was
probably one of the most beautiful women of her
age, and extremely clever and accomplished.
There is no doubt that a great intimacy existed
between her and Lord Melbourne, but he was quite
old enough to be her father, and was possessed of
great power of conversation, and I see no need
whatever to assume impropriety, and certainly
none was proved by creditable testimony. I have
recently read through the evidence very carefully,
and if I had been counsel for the defendant,
I should not have entertained any doubt of a successful result; indeed, I cannot understand how
her husband could have been so ill-advised as to
bring the action. Notwithstanding the ability of
Sir William Follett, the jury gave a verdict for the
defendant without the slightest hesitation. The
case was tried in the Court of Common Pleas, before
Sir Nicholas Tindal, a most painstaking judge. Mrs.
Norton herself felt very acutely the indignity she
had been subjected to, but society entirely absolved
her—a conclusion that I have heard was fully in-
dorsed by her Majesty, whose opinion must have
been a source of great comfort and satisfaction to
her in after-life.

However innocent Lord Melbourne may have
been, Sir John Campbell was not justified in stating

' that his client solemnly and upon his honour declared his innocence.' Most clients would do the
same if they could find counsel who would lend
themselves to repeating the assertion. Sir John
was at this time the leader of the bar, and this extremely unprofessional proceeding was not a good
example to his juniors. He certainly told the jury
in the same breath that they ought not to be
influenced by it. But Sir John was not a man to
waste his words.[1]

In the course of my subsequent career I was
frequently engaged in cases before Mr. Norton.
He was an extremely pleasant, gentlemanly man,
and a good magistrate.

---

[1] The following are the words of the Attorney-General, copied
from the report of the trial in the *Times* newspaper, dated June 23,
1836: ' I think it right, in the name of Lord Melbourne, to declare,
as he has instructed me to do in the most clear, emphatic, and solemn
manner, that he never had any criminal intercourse with Mrs. Norton,
nor had he done anything in the slightest degree to abuse the confidence of Mr. Norton. The jury were not to be swayed by this
declaration.'

CHAPTER XII.

LORD LYNDHURST.

LORD LYNDHURST, when I saw him upon the occasion I have related in a former chapter, was of advanced age, but possessed a singularly noble and prepossessing appearance. The intellect stamped upon his features was accompanied by an expression of kindliness, his voice was musical, his manner refined and courteous.

His Life has been written by Lord Campbell, and fully justified what he himself said when he heard that it was contemplated, that the prospect added another pang to death.[1] Although born at Massachusetts, it was whilst it was a loyal colony, and he was consequently a British citizen. His father, an artist, painted several pictures that obtained great reputation, amongst others one now in the National Gallery, the subject being the Death

---

[1] I quote the following passage from a criticism upon Lord Campbell's Lives of Lyndhurst and Brougham that appeared in the *Times* newspaper of April 3, 1869: 'All through the Lives we see Lord Campbell running a literary muck, striking right and left with so sublime an impartiality that scarcely a man he jostles in the crowd of public characters he threads escapes unharmed.'

of Lord Chatham. I am not aware whether it is considered a great work by connoisseurs. I do not myself like the treatment of the subject. According to all his contemporaries, Lord Lyndhurst, whilst at the bar, was a most brilliant and successful advocate. His powers were tested in a case in which, with Sir Charles Wetherall, he was retained for the defence of a certain Dr. Watson, charged with high treason. Upon reading the case, it is difficult to avoid wondering that, instead of indicting him for the capital offence, the officers of the Crown had not proceeded against him for sedition. Lord Lyndhurst was at that time Mr. Serjeant Copley, and it fell to his lot to sum up the case in favour of the accused, a duty which he performed with admirable skill and judgment. I do not myself think that even with inferior advocacy the facts would have warranted a conviction, although, in such cases, much depends upon the prepossessions of the jury, and it was doubtless from this knowledge that Mr. Serjeant Copley wound up his address with an elaborate but most eloquent and powerful appeal to them, entreating them to dismiss all prejudice from their minds, and be governed solely by a fair construction of the evidence. Lord Castlereagh, a very influential member of the Government, was upon the bench during the trial, and was greatly struck by the ability displayed by the counsel, and through his lordship's influence a seat in Parliament was obtained for him, and subsequently he was made Solicitor-General. The Government under which he accepted the post was a Tory one, and Mr. Serjeant Copley had always professed strong Liberal opinions. He had not, however, taken any part in politics, nor did he betray any confidence or trust. And whatever may have been the views of the party he joined, his performance of the duties of his office was consistent with the liberal sentiments that he had previously expressed.

My earliest recollection of him was when he was holding the office of Chief Baron of the Exchequer, and it was in that capacity that he pronounced judgment in the celebrated case of Small *v.* Attwood. This case involved many complicated facts, and the question was as to the falsity or truth of certain representations in relation to the qualities of a mine ; and although his decision was reversed in the House of Lords, it was admitted at the time to be a model of clearness, and I believe now that the conclusion he arrived at is considered to be sound law.

He did not hold the place of common law judge for long, but during that time gave satisfaction to the public and the bar, to which latter he was kind and considerate. The tendency of his

mind was always to the side of mercy. He aided
and encouraged an inexperienced advocate, and
was careful that a client should not suffer through
any deficiencies of counsel. It is told of him that
when he became Chancellor, and upon one occasion was describing the principles upon which he
selected a judge, he said, 'I look out for a
gentleman, and if he knows a little law so much
the better.' Sir William Bolland, who, I believe,
was the only one he made, certainly fulfilled the
former condition. With Lord Lyndhurst's subsequent career history has dealt, and with it I had no
acquaintance, except occasionally having listened
to some of his brilliant displays in the House of
Lords when in opposition to a Liberal ministry.

Sir Charles Wetherall, although engaged against
the Government in the case of Dr. Watson, was
one of the last specimens of a thorough Tory of
the oldest school. He was a very learned man,
and much respected for his conscientious adherence
to opinions that were getting much out of fashion;
but whilst strait-laced in his principles, his ideas
of dress were much the reverse; in fact, he was one
of the greatest slovens that ever walked, and it
was a wonder when he did walk how his clothes
and his body contrived to keep together. He was
Recorder of Bristol, where his High Church and
State views had not rendered him particularly

popular, and a story is told that during the Bristol riots he made his escape from the fury of the mob in the disguise of a clean shirt and a pair of braces.

Reverting to the case before the House of Lords, I ought not to pass over without a few words the name of Charles Austin. He was a distinguished lawyer and scholar, but latterly confined himself to parliamentary business, in which he attained immense success, and realised a large fortune. He did not add to the character of the profession by accepting numerous cases which he well knew he could not attend to. Doubtless they were delivered by solicitors who were aware of the risk they ran, and preferred taking it to the chance of his being retained against them. I cannot, however, think the practice was honourable or one that could be justified on any grounds whatever. Mr. Austin himself retired early from the profession, and, marrying the accomplished step-daughter of Charles Dance, the author of many comediettas, in the performance of which Madame Vestris, Liston, Mathews, Mrs. Orger, and others delighted the public, retired into Norfolk, his native county, took to rural pursuits, and became Chairman of Quarter Sessions, in which capacity he gave great dissatisfaction to the county gentry by not properly appreciating the enormity of poaching.

With Sir Fitzroy Kelly I early formed an acquaintance, and was upon intimate terms with him down to his death. He was a skilled lawyer, and most industrious, and, although not a brilliant speaker, earnest, forcible, and logical, and in cases involving technicalities and complicated details I never knew any one his superior; nothing ever disconcerted him or turned him from his point.

One of the best instances I can recall of his advocacy was when he was counsel for the London Docks in an information laid against that company by the Crown. I was with Sir A. Cockburn, then Attorney-General, for the prosecution. Nothing could be heavier than the subject, or more masterly than the way with which Kelly dealt with it. He was listened to by Court and jury with rapt attention, and the reply of the Attorney-General showed how much he felt the overwhelming power of his opponent. There was another case in which I remember him, and in which a defendant had great reason to be grateful for his advocacy.

This was a charge against a city merchant of wealth and position, named Zulueta, who was tried at the Old Bailey for trafficking in slaves, the only instance I fancy in which such an offence has been charged against an English citizen. The facts proved against him were very formidable, and the view taken by Mr. Justice Maule, the judge who tried him, was unfavourable. The jury debated for a considerable time, but ultimately returned a verdict of not guilty.

Kelly was very ambitious, and his election for Ipswich was on one occasion followed by a petition which was attended by a painful incident. I knew something of the circumstances. There had been a great deal of bribery, and a person named Pilgrim had been the principal agent of Kelly's party. He had been got out of the way, of which fact Kelly must have been aware. Charles Phillipps had undertaken to conduct the case for him, but, tempted by a fee elsewhere, had deserted it and left him to manage it himself; whilst doing this he was most improperly asked by a member of the committee if he knew anything about Pilgrim, and he answered that he did not. If his counsel had been asked such a question, he could, with truth, have answered in a similar manner. Kelly ought to have declined to answer at all, but of course the inference then would have been conclusive against him. But no sophistry can justify what he did. It is well known that Sir Walter Scott constantly denied that he was the author of ' Waverley,' justifying himself by saying that when impertinent questions were put to him he had a moral right to do so; but in all these cases it is the motive that colours the act. There is, however, no doubt that the question put upon this occasion was perfectly unjustifiable. Sir Fitzroy was subsequently much persecuted by a Mr. Wason, who had been his opponent upon the above occasion, but who failed in his efforts to do him any substantial injury.

Sir Fitzroy became Chief Baron upon the resignation of Sir Frederick Pollock. He was a most painstaking and conscientious judge, but latterly became tedious, and doubtlessly interfered with the progress of business. He died at an advanced age, and up to a few days before his death, when I saw him, was in full possession of his faculties, and exhibited the greatest cheerfulness.

Kelly presided at the Central Criminal Court upon the trial of a woman named Margaret Waters, charged with murder. The case was known as the baby-farming case, and the accused was found guilty. I prosecuted upon the part of the Crown, and although the details were very shocking, and the conviction perfectly proper, I should have been glad if the jury had given a more favourable verdict, and I did what I could to obtain a commutation of the sentence of death ; but Sir Fitzroy, although he had been a strenuous advocate for abolishing the punishment of death, would not interfere on this occasion, and the woman was executed.

There is no doubt, however, that a severe example was required, as the system pursued was horrible in the extreme.

Sir Fitzroy Kelly's appearance was very striking: he had a finely-chiselled face and regular features, with an intelligent forehead and lively bright eyes; his manner was somewhat artificial, and his demeanour, always courteous, was of the old school. He was very hospitable, and also went out a great deal into society, where his pleasant manners and varied information made him always welcome; by his death I lost a most kind and valued friend.

I ought, I think, before concluding this sketch, to mention a trial in which he was engaged whilst at the bar, and which entailed upon him, I think unjustly, a good deal of ridicule. This was the case of Tawell, a Quaker of eminent outward respectability, who, to maintain it, had poisoned a woman with whom he was connected, under circumstances of singular atrocity.

The poison indicated was prussic acid, and Sir Fitzroy accepted the suggestion of Dr. Letheby, the scientific chemist, that the odour discovered from the stomach of the deceased might have been caused by her eating apple-pips. The folly of the suggestion was due to Dr. Letheby, but I cannot approve of the judgment of the counsel in

accepting it. I shall have something to say hereafter of the opinions in such matters of professional
witnesses ; for the present I will only observe that,
whilst listened to with respect, they ought to be
adopted with great caution.

After I had been called some few years to the
bar, I was engaged in a case of some importance,
but of no interest to the public, and I only refer to
it for the purpose of introducing the name of Mr.
Justice James Alan Park, who presided upon that
occasion, for the last time before his death. He is
not unworthy of being remembered as a lawyer of
the old school, with prejudices of the oldest. I am
not sure whether he wore a pig-tail ; he ought to
have if he did not. He was singularly like his
Majesty George the Third, a fact of which he was
proud. He was called ' St. James's Park,' to distinguish him from the judge of the same name who
was called ' Green Park.' He was well versed in
the more abstruse branches of the profession, and
was generally respected by the public and the bar.
In his latter days he had acquired a habit of thinking aloud, which led on one occasion to a rather
amusing incident. Whilst trying an old woman
upon a charge of stealing faggots, he unconsciously
ejaculated, ' Why, one faggot is as like another
faggot as one egg is like another egg.' The counsel
defending the case heard the observation, and

repeated it to the jury. 'Stop,' said Sir James—
' stop ; it is an intervention of Providence. This
was the very thought that passed through my
mind. Gentlemen' (addressing the jury), 'acquit
the prisoner.'

I cannot resist telling a story, although it does
not say much for the decorum of the old Midland
Circuit, or of the eminent lawyers who practised
upon it in those days. Serjeants were then an institution, and the old Midland boasted of many
most learned and eminent ones : Goulburn, Clark,
Vaughan, Adams, Hayes, are no mean names, and
were all of this rank ; but those were times when
even serjeants were not always distinguished for
sobriety, and it so happened that upon one particular evening much conviviality had been indulged in, the merry party being congregated at
an hotel where the judge, Sir James Alan Park,
was staying. One of the body had escaped early,
and was supposed to have gone to bed, contrary
to all circuit rules ; it was determined to seek him,
and the whole party, with as much steadiness as
they could preserve, entered what they supposed
to be his bed-room, and jerked the clothes off the
bed of its sleeping occupant. Imagine their horror
when they were confronted with the venerable
countenance of the judge.

Their disappearance was quickly made, and

grave deliberations were entered into as to what was to be done, and it was determined that Serjeant Goulburn, a great favourite and friend of his lordship, should explain and apologise. Accordingly, next morning, with no small trepidation, he proceeded to do so, stating whom it was intended to have awakened. 'No, no,' said Sir James, shaking his head, ' brother Goulburn, it was no mistake, for I heard my brother Adams say, " Let us unearth the old fox." '

Many other tales are told of the merry days of a circuit that nevertheless produced some of the brightest ornaments of our profession, and upon whose records are inscribed names that will never perish—those of Copley and Denman.

CHAPTER XIII.

MR. BARON PARKE.

THE learned judge who obtained the sobriquet of Green Park, to distinguish him from Mr. Justice James Allan Parke, was one of the Barons of the Exchequer, and in my opinion no man ever held a place upon the bench with greater honour to himself and benefit to the public. Undoubtedly he had his defects, but in the higher attributes of his office he has never been surpassed.

Much of his character was reflected upon his countenance, which exhibited great power and intelligence. Upon the bench his deportment was grave without being in the slightest degree pompous. He paid the most profound attention to the proceedings, never exhibited signs of impatience, was courteous to every one alike, and would now and then go out of his way to say a kindly word of encouragement to a beginner. He was admitted to be a learned and accomplished lawyer, although accused of yielding his mind too much to the subtleties of the profession. He loved the law, and probably, like lovers of more material things,

could see no fault in the object of his love. His
tendency to uphold technical views gave rise to a
very clever squib by the late Mr. Justice Hayes, in
which the spirit of the baron is supposed to arrive
in Hades, where, instead of receiving the applause
that he expected from admiring ghosts, he is
mobbed by several of them, who had been obliged
to quit their earthly tenements before he had settled
a point really immaterial to their respective claims.

When late one day at a party, he told a lady
of my acquaintance that he could not tear himself
away from a beautiful demurrer. His fondness for
fresh air will long be remembered by those engaged
in some of the trials over which he presided. On
the coldest day in the early spring he insisted upon
every window of the court being open, and the jury,
each member with a different coloured handkerchief over his head, a shivering sheriff and despair-
ing Ordinary, presented a sufficiently comical scene
to those not too frozen to be amused by it. He was
occasionally in the habit of sitting until late in the
evening, which I am obliged to say I cannot altogether excuse, as very few of those engaged in a
cause had equal powers of endurance with himself.
He suffered fearfully from gout, but this never
affected his temper or impaired his faculties. Upon
his retirement from the bench he was created a
life peer, but objections being taken to the power

of the Crown to establish such an office, he received a peerage in the usual way, and was called up to the House of Lords under the title of Baron Wensleydale, and here he assisted most usefully upon the hearing of appeals. He might be seen of an afternoon wending his way to the House upon a roan cob, as grave and respectable in its deportment as its rider. He did not survive his promotion very long, and, leaving no male issue, the title became extinct.

Baron Parke presided in two cases on the Home Circuit in which I was engaged to defend the prisoners. They were both charges of murder: one was tried at Chelmsford, and the other at Lewes. I look back to them with considerable interest. They were the first in which I was counsel and where the life of a client was involved; and I think that the circumstances of both of them were such as to render them worth relating.

In the first case, a young woman of somewhat prepossessing appearance was charged with poisoning her husband. They were people in a humble class of life, and it was suggested that she had committed the act to obtain possession of money from a burial fund, and also that she was on terms of improper intimacy with a young man in the neighbourhood.

The solicitor instructing me was vehement in

expressing belief in his client's innocence. I was of a different opinion. He, acting upon his belief, desired that certain witnesses should be called. I, governed by my convictions, absolutely refused to do so, offering at the same time to return my brief. This, however, was refused, and I was left to exercise my own responsibility. The above question frequently arises, and some counsel have considered themselves bound to obey the wishes of the solicitor. There is no doubt that this is the safest course for the advocate, for if he does otherwise and the result is adverse he is likely to be much blamed, and the solicitor also is exposed to disagreeable comments; but I hold, and have always acted upon the opinion, that the client retains counsel's judgment, which he has no right to yield to the wishes or opinions of any one else. He is bound, if required, to return his brief, but if he acts against his own convictions he sacrifices, I think, his duty as an advocate. When the case came on, another incident occurred in which again I was called upon to exercise my view against the wishes of the solicitor. He desired that I should challenge one of the jurymen, but, not giving what I thought were valid grounds, I refused to do so, thinking then, and I have no reason since for considering otherwise, that using this privilege produces an unfavourable effect, and that it ought never to be exercised except upon very substantial grounds.

I do not propose to go through the details of the trial. It is sufficient to say that a minute quantity of arsenic was discovered in the body of the deceased, which in the defence I accounted for by the suggestion that poison had been used carelessly for the destruction of rats. Mr. Baron Parke summed up not unfavourably to the prisoner, dwelling pointedly upon the small quantity of arsenic found in the body, and the jury without much hesitation acquitted her, and, oddly enough, the juryman, whom it was suggested I should challenge, showed himself strongly in her favour throughout the trial. Dr. Taylor, the professor of chemistry, and an experienced witness, had proved the presence of arsenic, and, as I imagine, to the great disappointment of my solicitor, who desired a severe cross-examination, I did not ask him a single question. He was sitting on the bench and near the judge, who, after he had summed up and before the verdict was pronounced, remarked to him that he was surprised at the small amount of arsenic found; upon which Taylor said that if he had been asked the question he should have proved that it indicated, under the circumstances detailed in evidence, that a very large quantity had been taken.

The professor had learnt never to volunteer

evidence, and the counsel for the prosecution had omitted to put the necessary question. Mr. Baron Parke, having learnt the circumstance by accidental means, did not feel warranted in using the information, and I had my first lesson in the art of ' silent cross-examination.'

Some years after, at the Central Court, I was engaged in an unimportant trial, the prosecutrix of which was a comely middle-aged woman. The officer in the case told me that she was my old Chelmsford client. She had married her former lover, and they were keeping a public-house in the east end of London, under other names, and bore highly respectable characters.

On the outskirts of the town of Hastings, at the time of the occurrences I am about to relate—a time that my readers may guess when I tell them the railway had not extended beyond Tunbridge—there lived in a detached residence an elderly couple of respectable position. Their establishment consisted of two maid-servants and a housekeeper, who had for many years been a valued and trusted servant. A man whom we will call Smith—his real name has escaped my memory—had been footman, but had left some weeks before. It was upon a certain Sunday at this date that, according to their usual custom, the master and mistress and the two maid-servants had gone to morning church, leaving the

house in charge of the housekeeper. Upon their
return, shortly before one o'clock, they found the
old lady weltering in her blood, barbarously murdered. Plunder had evidently been the object, as
many articles were missing, and the poor creature
had probably met her fate endeavouring to protect
the property of her employers.

A reward was offered for the discovery of the
murderer, and in the result Smith was apprehended
and ultimately tried at the Lewes assizes before Mr.
Baron Parke, and I was retained for and defended
him.

. It appeared that upon the Saturday afternoon
preceding the murder he had been met in London by
an acquaintance, to whom he had applied for the loan
of some small sum of money. He told this person
that he was going to return to Hastings, and at about
half-past eleven o'clock on the Sunday morning he
passed through a turnpike gate upon the outskirts of
the town, and near to the house where the crime was
afterwards committed. He was well known to the
turnpike man, who proved this fact, and no doubt
was thrown upon the accuracy of these witnesses.
The subsequent evidence, if true, was conclusive of
his guilt, and yet partly through error and mis-
management by the police, and partly through
falsehood and exaggeration introduced by the
witnesses in hopes of the reward, it crumbled to

pieces, and I obtained an acquittal with the entire
concurrence of the judge, although neither he nor
I had the slightest doubt of the prisoner's guilt.

The first witness called was a cobbler, of a
religious turn of mind. He swore that he was
taking home a pair of boots to a customer, and
being ashamed to be seen pursuing carnal avocations on the Lord's day he had gone through some
fields behind the house where the murder took
place, and saw the prisoner entering by the back
way. Under cross-examination he speedily came
to grief. No one in court could doubt that his
evidence was utterly false. He could not tell who
his customer was, and as for the boots they were
perfectly mythical, and he was obliged to admit
that he had been very diligent in his inquiries
about the reward.

The stolen property was found under a hedge,
concealed in a pocket-handkerchief, which I have
no doubt whatever belonged to the prisoner,
and one of the maid-servants swore that she had
seen him using it when formerly he had been her
fellow-servant, but by way of making her evidence
more conclusive, pointed to a hole which she declared she noticed at that time. A washerwoman
from London was called also to speak to it. She
had washed it after he had left the service, and she
swore positively that there was no hole in it when

in her possession. Footsteps, identified by the police as the prisoner's, were said to have been discovered near the place where the property was found, but the gravest doubt was thrown upon this evidence by a riding-master, who declared that after the articles must have been deposited where they were found, and before the discovery, there had been a storm which, to use his own expression, would have washed out the hoof-marks of a horse; in truth, the whole of the evidence was tainted by the existence of a promised reward.

The discrepancies which were patent, and the undoubted falsehood told by the cobbler, were sufficient, in themselves, to wreck the case ; but another portion of the evidence produced failed in so singular a manner, that anything like a conviction was rendered impossible.

The prosecution undertook to prove that the prisoner was at a village between Tunbridge and Hastings called Robertsbridge on the night before the murder. This proof was obviously superfluous, as the evidence of the turnpike man was undisputed, and brought the prisoner conclusively upon the spot of the murder. But this endeavour gave rise to the most dramatic scene I ever witnessed in a court of justice. The postman of Robertsbridge swore positively to having met him, and, noticing that he was looking tired, invited him to come to a public-house and take a glass of ale; that he did so, and remained for some half-hour talking to him and three other persons, who corroborated this statement. None of them had the slightest doubt of his identity. Nor were they shaken by cross-examination. They not only recognised his person, but having heard him speak before the magistrate, stated that they remembered the tone of his voice. At my request a person was placed in the dock beside him. The postman was desired to look at the two then standing together. He trembled, turned ghastly pale, and I thought he would have fainted. The excitement in court was intense, and a pin might have been heard to drop. The likeness between the two men was marvellous; the postman looked and looked again; at last he gasped out, ' I do not know which is the man.' And, in fact, he had been mistaken; it was incontrovertibly shown that the man I produced was the person whom the postman had met. He had come down by the same train as the prisoner, and was on the way to Hastings at the time he was met at Robertsbridge. He had not appeared at the preliminary proceedings, not wishing, for family reasons, that his journey to and from London should be known. Thinking, however, that his silence might endanger the life of a fellow-creature, he had communicated with the prisoner's solicitor. Either the police

knew of his existence, in which case the Robertsbridge witnesses ought never to have been produced, or they must have been guilty of gross
negligence if they did not.

I have since endeavoured to find out what had
become of the accused man after his acquittal. I
heard that for a short time he had been guard to a
coach, but could learn nothing of his subsequent
career. The learned Baron had summed up the
case with his usual clearness and impartiality. The
jury did not debate for five minutes, and to illustrate a habit of the learned judge, to which I have
already alluded, when they were pronouncing the
verdict of ' not guilty ' a neighbouring clock was
tolling the hour of midnight.

CHAPTER XIV.

IMPRESSIONS OF SWITZERLAND AND HOMBURG.

MY readers will have discovered by this time, if I had not already told them, that whilst I pledge myself to the substantial accuracy of the facts I relate, I possess but little method in stating them. I rarely give dates, and make no attempt at chronological order ; all I seek is to reproduce impressions that were made upon me at the time of the occurrences to which they refer, and my opinions and thoughts upon them for whatever they may be worth, and thus, in defiance of all order, I travel from grave to trivial, and from matters of business to those merely of pleasure.

My last chapter might have been extracted from the 'Newgate Calendar.' I will now ask my readers to imagine a certain long vacation, and, quitting the region of crime, to accompany me upon a very unpretending excursion to what I have always thought the most beautiful of lands. My passport has been obtained, and I have without a sign of regret bidden adieu for the present to forensic costume, and am attired for foreign travel. Switzerland is my goal, and there I expect to meet my old friend, Albert Smith; it is the year after he has taken possession of Mont Blanc, and has laid the foundation of a fortune which, up to this time, had been coy to no unworthy courtship. For he was a man of genius, and, if inferior to Thackeray and Dickens, he was by no means wanting in the descriptive powers of the latter author. He possessed much sense of humour, and was capable of writing a story that maintained a strong interest throughout with the reader. As a companion he was full of fun, and bubbled over with high spirits. He had passed some years of his early life in Paris in the study of medicine, and could record many an amusing scene of the Quartier Latin. He spoke French fluently, and the good-looking, fair-haired young Englishman must have been a favoured partner at the dances, when grisettes, now a departed class, after the honest labour of the day, indulged in much joyousness without coarseness or crime.

One of his early productions was a novel called ' Mr. Ledbury's Tour.' It was extremely entertaining from the beginning to the end; the first volume contains some powerful writing; it also gives the account of an incident which happened when I was in his company. We were returning from some place of amusement, and were walking on the banks of the Seine close to the Pont Neuf, when we were startled by a splash. We saw a body in the stream about the centre under the bridge—only for a moment, and then the dark waters closed over it. On the following day the lifeless body of a good-looking young man, apparently English, was stretched out upon the slab of the Morgue. His dress betokened that he was of the better class. I never learnt any of the facts connected with the catastrophe, and do not know whether the account of the gambling-house scene introduced into 'Mr. Ledbury's Tour' has been founded upon any knowledge subsequently obtained of this unfortunate man's history.

I had engaged to meet my friend at Geneva, but will commence my tour at that well-known refuge for travellers the Trois Rois at Basle. Fancy that I am standing in its spacious hall, awaiting the decision of a grave official as to whether I shall be allowed to enter farther within its precincts. I am at last invited to climb a number of stairs, fit preparation for mountain travel, and am assigned a few feet of uncarpeted floor with a tiny bed, but sheets very tempting in their whiteness. I hear a rushing noise, and looking out of the little window of my room I see for the first time the broad expanse of the Rhine hastening upon its downward voyage to the ocean.

It was long before I could tear myself from the view of the mighty river. It was an autumn evening, and a moon nearly at its full was silvering the waters as they careered along, whilst small lights began to show themselves from the gabled buildings on the opposite side, and, when I cast my eyes up the stream, the hills but dimly seen furnished the imagination with a glorious promise of beauty and grandeur.

I descend into the well-known *salon*. The *table d'hôte* is over, and the tables are laid out for tea; everything looks fresh. Honey, the prominent feature of the tea-table, tempts to a beverage of which the innocence is in keeping with the purity of the scene.

There is a balcony outside running the entire length of the room; it is here that Anthony Trollope has fixed the locality of one of his charming love-scenes. And where could be found a better? The warm soft feeling of an early autumn evening, the moon upon the waters, the music of the stream —all these, perchance, as new sensations as the words of a first love whispered in their presence.

Let us now go to the front of the hotel, where in those days was witnessed a sight that will never be seen there again—a large open space filled with carriages of every description, and coachmen in every guise, the tinkling of bells, and now and again the loud cracking of whips, which secure a space for travelling-carriages to dash up to the door, where an obsequious porter receives the inmates. The conveyances waiting around have deposited their freights, and their drivers are looking out for the chance of a party return- ing to the localities to which they respectively belong.

Now all is changed. The railway disgorges its hundreds at fixed times. The only vehicles to be seen are the unromantic omnibuses, and a miscel- laneous crowd hustle their way into the hotel, their object apparently being to visit the greatest num- ber of places in the shortest possible period; the most earnest inquiries generally being about the time that the next train will start.

The Rhine still pursues its downward course from the mountains. The Trois Rois stands where it did, the same official disposes of the human mass, but instead of the groups that one remembers dwell- ing with newly awakened sensations of pleasure at a beautiful and novel scene, and viewing with in- terest the curiosities of the country which orna- ment the saloons, there appears to have sprung up a feeling of indifference. 'Move on, move on,' seems to be the cry. The crack of the postilion's whip and the jingling bells of the horses are no longer heard; they have been superseded by the scream of the steam engine, and the traveller, hot and almost suffocated by the closeness of the railway carriage, passes in a semi-comatose state through the most lovely and glorious of nature's works. From Basle I went to Zurich, sharing a carriage with two travellers whom I accidentally met. A charming drive it was ; it is now accomplished by train. And upon this journey it was that for the first time a range of snow-clad mountains presented themselves to my wondering eyes, a sight, indeed, that surpassed everything that my imagination had pictured. From Zurich I hastened on to Geneva, where, at one of the hotels in the town—the palaces since built did not then exist—I met my friend Albert Smith and his brother Arthur, and with them innocently amused myself by catching small fish and admiring the exquisite scenery of the lake. After a day or two I accompanied them to Chamouni, where I profited by the celebrity that they had acquired. It is sad to think that none of us will ever hear again the story told by Albert of his ascent of the great mountain. His pleasant voice and manner and really graphic description of the incidents gave it a great charm, and his intro-duction, under the title of 'Galignani's Messenger,' of a topical song, was a great success. The prettily ornamented room at the Egyptian Hall was nightly filled, and the amusement afforded was of a kind that offered no impediment to the presence of the most strait-laced of moralists.

In returning from Geneva I passed over the Jura, one of the most lovely ranges of mountains in Switzerland, now lost to the traveller in consequence of the railway. From the banquette of the diligence each turn of the road presented a new scene of beauty to its occupier. Having reached Dijon, at which place we stopped, the journey home was shortly accomplished. I cannot imagine that the impression made by this my first visit to Switzerland will ever be effaced.

A very different place, dependent more upon art than natural beauty, although by no means deficient in the latter quality, was Homburg. Sparkling it was and brilliant when I first knew it, which was a long time ago. Its beauties and its naughtinesses have been often described.

How joyous was the scene it presented in the early morning, and who would guess that any of the gaily dressed throng crowding round the springs were invalids in search of health! Everything was there that could enliven. The crisp air, through which vibrated the lively strains of music, gave freshness to the charms of the scene. What a place for a gossip, or for a flirtation! Dangerous, I admit, for under such influences words may be spoken not easily, if repented, to be recalled.

Those seats with honeysuckles and jasmine twining around the trellis-work have, I will venture to say, been the scene of many a vow breathed, and many a soft response. Then the parade, shaded on each side by trees, was crowded with company exchanging friendly salutes as they sauntered from one spring to the other. The visitors on the occasion I am now thinking of were principally English, most of them well known in the world of fame and fashion. I could mention the names of many ladies, but it would be invidious to select among so much that was beautiful in the fair sex any particular example.

Amongst the men one figure might every morning be seen striding manfully along, battling gallantly with an old enemy, the gout, recognising with a kindly nod and smile those whom he knew —and they were many, for with one of the known characteristics of his family he never forgot a face. This was the Duke of Cambridge, who annually sought these springs, and was always an object of interest to his fellow-countrymen. Another visitor, seen also frequently leaning upon a gentleman's arm and pacing slowly up and down, was the Grand Duke of Mecklenburg Strelitz, the blind prince, his great calamity making him the object of compassion, whilst the courage with which he bore it obtained for him feelings of admiration and respect. It was my great privilege to join some

small parties in which he entertained many affectionate friends, and in the course of which he displayed qualities proving that his grievous calamity
had in no respect impaired his power of feeling as
well as of imparting intellectual enjoyment. It
was during this visit to Homburg that I had the
honour of being introduced to his Royal Highness
the Prince of Wales, from whom since that time I
have met with many instances of kindly feeling. In
the evening, after the cafés and hotels had, in some
instances, furnished reasonably good dinners, a
different scene was presented in another locality.
On a terrace outside the conversation rooms were
numerous tables, seated at which the visitors were
enjoying coffee, ices, and no small quantity of beer.
They were composed of all ranks, ladies of the
highest, in costumes of exquisite taste, mingling
with the peasantry from the surrounding country,
decked in their village finery ; and mixing amongst
the crowd was to be met the flashily dressed
tradesman from Frankfort, and the unlucky gambler
who had just lost his last napoleon. A fine band
played a succession of popular airs, and thus the
evening afforded a fund of amusement to those
content to enjoy the natural beauties of the place
and the means of enhancing them so liberally
supplied by the proprietor of the gambling establishment. There were occasional operas, at

which Patti delighted the visitors, and the drives
in the surrounding woods afforded both health and
pleasure in the daytime to those who preferred to
seek them to the fascinations presented in the gorgeous saloons of the establishment. It was in these
that the naughtinesses prevailed. I wish I was
able to speak of them with becoming reprobation,
but prefer to leave this office to others better qualified to do so.

No doubt all the evil passions which are supposed to emanate from a certain place were present
at the gambling tables, but there was such an air
of decorum that they were concealed from an
ordinary observer. A serious lady of my acquaintance called it a feast of Satan; but the
attendants upon the banquet were so decently clad,
and conducted themselves so quietly, and looked
altogether so very respectable, that it was difficult
to take them for that gentleman's satellites. Still,
the word of the moralist went forth : Homburg
was purified and gambling driven into holes and
corners where there is no supervision to prevent
the worst of frauds, or else it has a decent coat
put on and is called speculation.

I wonder whether Monsieur Blanc in his splendid palaces, with his *refaits* and zeros, has broken
more hearts and disseminated more ruin than that
scrupulously washed and dressed gentleman whom

on a Sunday you may see walking so decorously to church, who occupies two dirty rooms in Throgmorton Street, and is a shareholder in that mighty gambling house the Stock Exchange.

Before bidding adieu to Homburg it is only right to say that everything was conducted with perfect fairness. No imputation to the contrary has ever been suggested. Every one knew or might have known the chances secured to the tables. No one could fail to see around him, in the amusements and luxuries provided by the proprietor for the visitors, proof of the enormous profits he must be realising; and, independently of the advantages incident to the tables, the most important of which was the limit that players were restricted to, and which almost without an exception could beat the capitalist, whilst the funds of the bank defeated the smaller speculators—it really was a machine working uninfluenced by passion or feeling against those who were operated upon intensely by both.

Most of the *habitués* practised a system, but I never yet knew of a case in which it succeeded for any length of time, although I have heard and known of large sums won by strokes of luck where the player has succeeded without any pretence to science or calculation. Around the table, and wandering listlessly about the rooms, might be seen shabbily dressed individuals, apparently without an object on earth : they are ruined gamblers —the passion still strong upon them, the means of gratifying it departed. You might sometimes see one of these individuals move stealthily up to an apparent novice, and suggest to him that for a few florins he could teach him an invaluable mode of play. If the novice listens to him he will explain the mere accident which prevented his own success. Perhaps he obtains what would get him one decent meal, but with flushed face he creeps to the roulette table, puts the piece upon his favourite number, with a haggard smile upon his face sees it swept off by the croupier, and steals back penniless and starving, to continue his hopeless wanderings.

An observer might also notice certain ladies who, whatever might be their character, are quiet and unobtrusive. When first seen they shine with much jewellery : this from day to day diminishes, and finally the whole has disappeared.

I do not fail to remember that Mr. Goldsmidt, the obliging banker, in High Street, had always some diamonds that he could sell you, 'a very great bargain.'

The countenances of the visitors departing from Homburg are graver than they were when starting to reach it. It is to be hoped that enough remains in their pockets to secure a meal at the Hôtel de

Russie at Frankfort, which, if anything can do it, will restore their cheerfulness. Stories are told of the hotel keepers at Homburg having some specific by which they find out when their customers are ruined, and furnish them with means to take their unlucky carcases to some other locality, where they may dispose of them as they please.

Upon one occasion I must own to having been guilty of a very unjustifiable ruse to get possession of a seat at the rouge-et-noir table. It was occupied by a lady well known at the springs: she was of the highest respectability, and although she could not resist the temptation of play, she indulged in it upon thoroughly economic principles, making three or four crown pieces last for a considerable time. She was not young, she was not beautiful, and was very jealous of her husband, which was a fact pretty notorious. Well, there, upon one occasion, she was sitting staking a crown about every half hour, and, having five crowns left, she had evidently capital enough upon this system to last the entire day. I looked around; no vacancy seemed likely to be made by other players, and so it occurred to me, moved, as we say in the criminal courts, by the instigation of the devil, to say to a friend, loud enough for her to hear, 'I wonder who that pretty girl is that Charlie—— is flirting with on the parade,' naming her spouse. The legs of her chair grated upon the ground as it was drawn rapidly back; the five crowns were swept together and deposited in her reticule, and hastily and anxiously the lady departed. I trust I may be forgiven, and I am glad to say that I heard of no domestic calamity.

One other little incident I cannot forbear relating. There was a well-known frequenter of the rooms—I will furnish her with a fancy name. Mrs. Delamere was an elderly female, with a countenance that did not attract, and who certainly could not be charged with using any meretricious ornament. She took her seat daily at the roulette table : with much diving into a bag she would produce her capital, six or seven florins being apparently its limit. She secured a chair early, and kept it resolutely against all comers, watching the chances of the table. The incident I am about to relate will show what she considered them to be. One day there entered the rooms a lady of a type very different from that of the ordinary frequenters. She was clad in a sober dark dress, almost quaker-like in its neatness. A bonnet that at once established the respectability of its wearer surmounted a middle-aged and not unpleasing countenance. The stranger seemed fascinated by the tables ; she approached them, walked round them, peeped over the players' heads, and after an evident inward struggle placed a napoleon upon a number immediately in front of Mrs. Delamere. Round went the wheel, and to that number thirty-five napoleons were pushed by the croupier. These Mrs. Delamere immediately clutched. The lady to whom they belonged mildly expostulated, saying they were hers. 'Yours!' yelled Mrs. D., looking her victim sternly in the face. 'Don't try that game with me—this is not the first time you have attempted it.' The lady shrank back abashed, and Mrs. Delamere thus became an instrument in the hands of Providence to check, at its very outset, a tendency to the debasing vice of gambling in a fellow-creature.

Homburg is still charming, and still attracts. The springs are, as formerly, crowded in the morning, and on my last visit I recognised many old faces. The band still played ; the same mixed crowd was to be seen in the evening ; and it certainly had this advantage, to those who studied economy but were unable to resist temptation, that it was much cheaper than in former days.

At Monaco there still exists an establishment in which, in one of the most lovely spots in the world, rouge-et-noir and roulette are played with every circumstance of outward decorum. It is said that the prince of the country derives his principal revenue from the proprietors. Lately a movement has been got up by certain English sojourners to procure their expulsion. A friend of mine, who possesses a very beautiful villa in the neighbourhood, was solicited the other day by another resident to sign a memorial for this purpose, but as he considered that those who did not like it might keep away, and that it was pure impertinence to interfere with the arrangements of a foreign place, he absolutely declined. His friend exhausted every argument upon the score of morals without avail, and, making a last effort, he pointed out how much it would increase the value of their property. I should be very sorry to treat with disrespect the conscientious scruples of any class, and, if pressure comes from the natives of a country to abolish an institution, it ought to be treated with consideration; but really the opinions of foreigners who might find plenty of improprieties in their own country to reform, are, in my humble judgment, worthy not only of no attention, but are generally the outcomings of self-interest, and signal examples of impertinence and conceit.

CHAPTER XV.

LORD CAMPBELL.

In the year 1850 Lord Denman, stricken by illness, retired from the bench. If not so profound a lawyer as some of those who had filled the office of Lord Chief Justice in former years, he possessed the highest qualities of a great judge, and the necessity for his retirement occasioned general regret, and a more complete contrast can scarcely be imagined than that presented between him and his successor, Lord Campbell. The high-minded feeling and heartfelt courtesy of the one was replaced by a superficial veneer of forced politeness, that concealed the natural bad taste and peevish temper of the other.

I have indicated in former pages the importance I attach to the demeanour of a judge when upon the bench. He has no excuse for discourtesy, he naturally commands the respect and consideration of all present. Fractiousness and impatience seriously impair his usefulness. They produce nervousness in counsel of inexperience, who ought to be encouraged, if not out of kindness to themselves, for the sake of those to whom it is the duty of the judge to see, to the best of his power, that justice is done. Lord Campbell was a learned and skilled lawyer, but his manner was harsh and irritable. He had no compassion for weakness. He crushed where he ought to have striven to raise. It is of no value for a sufferer to be told, even if it be the fact, that under an offensive demeanour there exist a kind heart and amiable disposition; such knowledge affords no comfort to a young barrister who has been snubbed before his first client and the entire court. Lord Campbell ought to have had mercy, for he was by no means himself insensible to applause, and sometimes sought it by not very dignified means. His Life, unlike the Lives of those whose history he has written, has been delivered to posterity by himself, and he escaped the death-pang that others, not without reason, apprehended from his undertaking their biography.

He undoubtedly was a consistent partisan, and his views were enlarged and liberal upon the great political subjects with which he had to deal; at the same time it must be admitted that the services he performed met with sufficiently substantial rewards, and his Diaries show that he pursued his material interests with skill and unflagging perseverance. He obtained a peerage for his wife as a consideration for remaining Attorney-General at a time when his resignation of that office would have been of serious inconvenience to the Ministry ; and when, in 1841, the Government to which he was attached was tottering, he created a scandal by securing to himself the appointment of Irish Lord Chancellor and a peerage. His services in that capacity lasted about a fortnight—a fact that the long-headed Scotchman must have foreseen. When the vacancy occurred in the Chief Justiceship, it was only proper that he should obtain a post which not only his services but his great legal attainments fully entitled him to. And of his subsequent appointment as Chancellor there is no reason to complain. I do not know whether he was popular with the equity bar, or what judgment was formed of his ability in that branch of the law, but he certainly possessed the merit of unwearying industry, and exhibited upon all occasions a conscientious endeavour to make himself master of his subject.

His Lives of the Chancellors and Chief Justices are pleasant and readable books, and exhibit his love for work, although he by no means disdained to avail himself of the labours of others, which I do not remember that he ever acknowledged. I heard Charles Phillipps tell a story of having been talking to Lord Brougham at the House of Lords, when he pointed out to him an elderly female in a poke bonnet standing at the bar. ' Do you see,' said he to Phillipps, ' the old lady standing there? She is Miss Strickland. She is waiting to reproach Campbell with his literary larcenies. He will escape by the back way.' It appears, however, from an extract that I insert from his Diary, that he was not successful in doing so. The following is his account of, I presume, the occurrence related by Phillipps :—

' My exploit in the House of Lords last night was introducing myself to Miss Strickland, authoress of the " Lives of the Queens of England," who has been writing a violent letter against me in the newspapers. After I had conversed with her for half an hour, she exclaimed, " Well, Lord Campbell, I do declare you are the most amiable man I ever met with." I thought Lord Brougham would have died with envy when I told him the result of my interview; and Ellenborough, who was sitting by, rubbed his hands in admiration. Brougham had thrown me a note across the table saying, " Do you know that your friend Miss Strickland is come to hear you ? " '

I suspect that, if it had been possible to have heard Lord Brougham's account of the interview, if indeed he witnessed it, more amusement would have been afforded to the reader than that transmitted to posterity by the most amiable man Miss Strickland ever knew.

Whilst he was at the bar, I had not many opportunities of hearing Campbell. He was, beyond doubt, a very skilful advocate. His manner was dry and not pleasing, but he commanded attention, possessed great power and force, and was, I should think, with rare exceptions, thoroughly judicious. In strictly legal arguments few men at the bar surpassed him, although Kelly was equally earnest and as well versed in legal subtleties; Follett, with certainly equal attainments, possessed a more fascinating voice and manner.

I have already given some account of the case of Norton v. Lord Melbourne, of the result of which Lord Campbell was very proud; but he has succeeded in many cases of far greater difficulty, though not of such public interest.

There was another case in which he was engaged, which also attracted a great deal of attention, and it so happened that my old master, the General, as Watson was always called, was engaged in it. The day before it came on I was dining with him, and the following morning I accompanied him to the Court of Queen's Bench, where it was tried before Lord Denman. It was an action brought by a Lord de Ros against a gentleman named Cumming for defamation, and Watson was with Thesiger and Alexander for the defence. It arose out of play transactions at different clubs, and it was alleged that Lord de Ros had been habitually guilty of cheating. The court was crowded to the ceiling, and I remember Lord Lyndhurst, amongst many other gentlemen, being upon the bench, taking apparently a great interest in the trial.

The story was a very strange one. Lord de Ros was a man of high family, I believe Senior Baron, and was not only a popular man, but wealthy and liberal in the ordinary transactions of every-day life, and a member of several of the best clubs in London and elsewhere. There was no doubt that, long before the matter was brought to an issue, whispers had circulated imputing to his lordship unfair practices. He had received a well-meant although anonymous communication advising him to desist from play, and a paragraph charging him broadly with cheating had appeared in a newspaper. Ultimately certain gentlemen, amongst whom was Mr. Cumming, undertook the responsibility of the charge, upon which the action was brought against him. The transactions attributed were alleged to have occurred at a club at Brighton, the Travellers', in Pall Mall, and more markedly at a proprietary club that was then in existence, and kept by a gentleman named Graham, and of which many distinguished men, including Lord de Ros, were members.

His lordship was an excellent whist player, and considered quite a match for the finest of the day. Nevertheless, it was asserted that he resorted to an elaborate trick to obtain an unfair advantage. I will endeavour to explain its nature, but it is difficult to do so clearly. It consisted in a reversal of the cut, that is to say, that after the cards had been cut to the dealer he would contrive, by an act of legerdemain, to replace the last card, which ought of course to have gone amongst the other cards, into its original position at the bottom of the pack. It is obvious that for the purpose of rendering this trick of benefit to the dealer he must have acquired a knowledge of what the card so replaced was. And it was said that for this purpose Lord de Ros contrived to mark certain court cards in such a manner as to be able to distinguish them and secure the presence of one of them at the bottom of the pack when he presented it to his adversary to be cut.

It is really incredible that any sane man should have conducted his proceedings with such recklessness as he did, and one cannot help thinking of the saying, 'Quem Deus vult perdere prius dementat.'

The witnesses examined against him had noticed that when about to deal he endeavoured to distract attention by coughing, an infirmity that did

not trouble him at other times, and one of them,
Sir William Ingelby, declared that he did not
remember an instance of his dealing without turning up a king or an ace; and the cards with which
he played were afterwards examined and found
to be marked, apparently with the thumb nail.
Colonel Anson, George Payne, and Lord Henry
Bentinck were amongst the witnesses deposing to
having noticed Lord de Ros in his mode of dealing.

These gentlemen were amongst the finest
players of the day, and he must have known that
they were looking on whilst he was transposing the
cards, which adds to his extraordinary folly, if it
does not almost prove him to have been insane.

Sir John Campbell, who with Sir William Follett and Mr. Wightman appeared for Lord de Ros,
made a long, energetic, and powerful speech, showing his capacity in a hopeless case. I cannot,
however, think that a suggestion he made of conspiracy upon the part of the gentlemen called could
be either prudent or justifiable, as it was clear that
they had all come forward most unwillingly. After
an anxious and thoroughly impartial charge by the
Lord Chief Justice, the jury, without hesitation,
found the only possible verdict, for the defendant.

The trick was not a new one, and was known
by the name of *sauter le coup*, and Sir William

Ingelby excited much laughter by undertaking with a pack of cards to show the mode in which it was performed, and, fortunately for his reputation, he made a very clumsy exhibition of it. Sir John Campbell also caused a good deal of fun by inadvertently describing it as *couper la saute*. An anecdote was related in connection with this case of a young member of the club who had noticed Lord de Ros performing this trick asking an older member what he ought to do. ' Bet upon him ' was the advice given, of course in joke.

An endeavour was made to show that Lord de Ros had some physical infirmity connected with the muscles of the hand, which would have prevented his manipulating the cards in the manner described, and for this purpose the eminent surgeon, Mr. Lawrence, was called, but did not succeed in substantiating this view. Mr. Lawrence was a skilful surgeon, and also a literary man of great attainment. He wrote a work in early life which was said to be anti-Christian, and he lost position with the public in consequence of it. The views enunciated in it are now to be found in the common literature of the day, but in those times freethought, or rather the expression of it, met with scant favour. I frequently met Mr. Lawrence during the latter days of his life, in professional matters. He laid himself open to be a witness in cases of railway accidents, but although his appearance was greatly in his favour, and his knowledge deep and varied, he was too hasty in forming an opinion, and too dogmatic in asserting it. I always thought it dangerous to call him, and preferred his being on the opposite side.

Of Sir William Follett, who was counsel both in this and the Melbourne trial, I knew personally but very little. From what I did know I should say no man ever lived more thoroughly unaffected or with a kinder heart, and of the greatness of his attainments all were agreed. Once only, when junior to Sir Frederick Pollock, I was opposed to him. In the absence of my leader a somewhat complicated verdict was returned, and Sir William, seeing my difficulty, helped me out of it. He had never spoken to me before, or I to him. His early death was a great source of sorrow to his private friends, and a very grave one to his country.

Mr. Wightman afterwards became one of the judges of the Court of Queen's Bench, and a very efficient and useful one. He had a certain amount of dry humour, an instance of which I remember upon a trial at the Maidstone assizes. A very excellent and learned friend of mine, not however famed for his brevity, had been for some considerable time enforcing his arguments before a Kentish jury. Mr. Justice Wightman, interposing, said,

' Mr. ———, you have stated that before,' and then, pausing for a moment, added, ' but you may have forgotten it, it was a very long time ago.' I have been before this judge very often, and have a very pleasant recollection of his courtesy and good humour, and his shrewdness was very formidable to a guilty client.

I only remember being present at one other case which Sir John Campbell, then Attorney-General, conducted. This was an indictment at the Central Court against a solicitor named Williams upon a charge of forging a will. Campbell was for the defence, and I followed his conduct of the case with great interest and attention, and certainly it was a fine specimen of powerful advocacy, and, against the view I had formed, it was successful. The prosecution gave rise to much subsequent litigation in our courts, which, however, as I believe, ended in the establishment of the will.

CHAPTER XVI.

CAMPBELL'S IRRITABILITY.

I HAVE not hesitated to express my opinion of
Lord Campbell's demeanour upon the Bench ; but
his great knowledge and unwearying industry rendered him an extremely powerful common law
judge. There is no doubt that a very learned man
in his position may feel weariness at the occasional
prolixity of counsel, but it is not less his duty to
restrain the exhibition of it where the advocate is
genuinely endeavouring to convey his views. The
impatience occasionally exhibited by Lord Campbell took a form at times that was positively gro-
tesque. I remember upon one occasion, during the
speech of a very able counsel, now a judge, that
after having shown many signs of irritability, his
lordship could no longer keep his seat, but, getting
up, marched up and down the bench, casting at intervals the most furious glances at the imperturb-
able counsel, and at last, folding his arms across
his face, leant as if in absolute despair against the
wall, presenting a not inconsiderable amount of back

O 2

surface to the audience.   A very clever caricature
was drawn of him by a barrister, representing his
half-dozen phases of disgust, and terminating with
his dorsal exhibition.

In 1856 he presided at the Central Court upon
the trial of William Palmer, upon a charge of murder.   This case was peculiarly one of cold-blooded
crime.   Palmer was by profession a surgeon, by
practice an assassin, and he was tried for poisoning
a person named John Parsons Cook

Sir Alexander Cockburn conducted the prosecution, admittedly in the very highest style of excellence.   Palmer was defended by Mr. Serjeant Shee,
a man of power and eloquence, and very earnest
and conscientious.   He was induced, and I am sure
with sincere conviction, to express a personal belief
that the accused was innocent, meaning, however,
merely that he was not guilty of committing the
crime by the agency suggested.   Lord Campbell
did not check or reprove him, probably having
Lord Melbourne's case in his recollection, and not
wishing to be reminded of it.   The prosecution
based their theory mainly upon the death having
been caused by strychnine ; which was founded
upon descriptions given by different witnesses of
the appearances the deceased exhibited before his
death.

There were, however, circumstances that weakened this theory, and certainly antimony had also been employed. Professor Taylor was very confident upon the subject; and attributed the death solely to the former poison, and if the case had been allowed to drift into chemical refinements, serious difficulties might have arisen. Sir Benjamin Brodie would give no opinion as to the actual poison used, but declared without hesitation that he had never known a natural death attended with the appearances described. The strong good sense of Lord Campbell brushed away the merely scientific question; showed that it was not material to discover by what poison the deed had been effected; dwelt with overwhelming force upon the facts, to which, as he explained, the medical evidence was merely subsidiary, and only used for the purpose of demonstrating that the appearances presented were consistent with the means suggested. I have no doubt that Palmer was a practised poisoner, and that he had hoped to evade justice by mingling the poisons and deceiving the scientific witnesses. If this was his aim, Lord Campbell signally defeated it.

He was convicted without much hesitation, and received his doom with perfect calmness. He was a sporting man, and when the verdict was returned wrote upon a slip of paper which he handed to his attorney, 'The riding did it,' alluding to Cockburn's speech.

Mr. Serjeant Shee had an impossible task. He was an old companion of mine upon circuit, and when Lord Denman appointed me a revising barrister I was associated with him as a colleague. He was subsequently made a judge of the Queen's Bench, the first Roman Catholic of late years appointed to that post in England, but did not survive his honours very long. He was highly esteemed and respected, especially by his brethren at the bar.

The reputation of Lord Campbell for politeness was amusingly illustrated by a remark made by the crier of the court to a friend at the commencement of this case. His lordship had said with great suavity of manner, 'Let the prisoner be accommodated with a chair.' 'He means to hang him,' said the crier.

History, it is said, repeats itself, and crime is no unimportant part of history, and will be found much the same, although in various disguises, in different generations. The motives actuating its commission, and the character of the criminal, can be clearly traced and recognised, but the modes by which the deed is accomplished vary with the period. Thus there is a close analogy between Palmer and a murderer named Thurtell, who was convicted some half-century ago. Both were called gentlemen: Thurtell, because he kept a gig ; Palmer, because he kept an apothecary's shop. Both were turfmen and gamblers. In both instances the victim was a particular friend and intimate associate of the murderer ; and in both, the object of the crime was to get rid of debts incurred at play or by betting. Thurtell's crime represented the coarseness of the age ; Palmer's, its improved intelligence. Had the former lived in Palmer's time, instead of first shooting and then battering out the brains of Weare, he would have invited his friend to supper, and put strychnine or antimony into the apple-sauce accompanying the roast pork of which that supper consisted, and with which Thurtell and his accomplices regaled themselves after the murder.

I dare say few of this generation recollect anything about the circumstances of the case to which I have referred.

Thurtell had lost money to Weare, and got an accomplice named Probert to ask him to a cottage belonging to that person down in Hertfordshire, and he himself undertook to drive him. In a lane near their destination, Thurtell drew a pistol and shot Weare in the head ; the wound not being fatal, he finished his work with the barrel of the pistol. The body was conveyed to Probert's cottage and deposited under a sofa, whilst a party, consisting of the owner of the cottage, Thurtell, a man named Hunt, and Probert's wife, had supper. The body was afterwards deposited in a pond, where it was subsequently found through the information of accomplices.

Probert and Hunt turned king's evidence. The former was subsequently hanged for what in any other person would have been treated as borrowing a horse, but the jury were only too glad to make him pay the penalty of his former crime. Hunt was transported, and I have heard was killed by the crew upon his outward voyage.

I remember two causes in which I was engaged before Lord Campbell : they were both founded upon railway accidents, and in both of them, through no fault of the judge, there was a miscarriage of justice; and although not of any great public interest, they illustrate some of the phases that present themselves, in actions of this kind, where the verdict depends not upon a question of fact, but upon the character of an admitted injury and the amount of compensation to be awarded. If such injury is outwardly apparent and none is said to exist internally, the task is not difficult, but almost in every case some occult evil is said to have occurred, sometimes without any foundation, and nearly always exaggerated, and a jury are obliged to rely upon the truthfulness of a claimant and the accuracy and sound judgment of professional men. It is somewhat unfortunate that many undoubtedly able medical men have made this class of case a specialty, and some of these gentlemen are almost invariably selected as witnesses, and I fear quite unwittingly act too often with a spirit of partisanship.

A gentleman named Glover was the plaintiff in the first of the two cases to which I have called attention. He had been, I believe, member for Reading, and, although no external injury was apparent, it was stated that he had received a serious spinal shock, and that the result might be fatal. His appearance, however, in the witness-box did not support this idea, and his manner prejudiced his case exceedingly. It was finikin and coxcombical, and many, of whom I confess myself to have been amongst the number, thought that he was not candid in giving his evidence; and the statements of the doctors, which gave a very grave aspect to the alleged symptoms, had in consequence less weight than they deserved. Lord Campbell took an unfavourable view, and evidently thought that there was gross exaggeration. The jury, coinciding in this opinion, returned a verdict quite inadequate to the injuries if truly represented. Within three months the unfortunate gentleman, a comparatively young man, died, and it could not be doubted that his premature death resulted from the effects of the injuries he had undergone, and which had been correctly indicated by the medical men.

I have, in a former chapter, whilst considering the mode of treating witnesses, cautioned an observer against being too much biassed by appearances, not necessarily indicative of a desire to deceive, but resulting from the natural infirmities of the human mind which become developed by the nervousness of an unaccustomed position, and I have seen a thoroughly honest witness show himself from this cause in a very unfavourable light.

In the other case, tried, I believe, before the same judge, the plaintiff was brought into court apparently in a moribund state. He seemed scarcely able to articulate, and his limbs were without power or sensibility. According to the doctors, and I do not impugn their truth as to the fact, his powers of sensation had been tested by a needle, which had been inserted in his arm without his exhibiting any sign of feeling; in fact, he created general sympathy, and obtained a very large verdict amounting to many thousands. It was thought useless to move for a new trial. Within a week after the time had elapsed for doing so the plaintiff was recognised climbing Snowdon in full activity and strength, and within the twelvemonth was presented with an heir, who, thanks to his father having been so nearly killed, was likely to have something to inherit.

The manufacturing of injuries has become a regular trade amongst a low class of practitioners— men who, although utterly ignorant of the elements of their profession, have had no difficulty in learning what are the usual symptoms of a grave shock. The patient is sometimes a rogue, and deliberately misrepresents his feelings. Sometimes the nervousness that follows a railway collision leads him readily to embrace ideas suggested by questions put to him by his attendant. The doctor has probably made a bargain by which he will secure to himself a percentage upon the damages awarded by the jury, which amount, the action being against a railway company, is certain to be paid.

There is a specimen of this kind of medical man well known in our courts. When last I saw him he would not swear that he had not been the doctor in more than one hundred cases arising from railway accidents, and he certainly could not have been selected for his knowledge, as he was unable to tell the normal temperature of the human body. It is not likely that a majority of general practitioners have legitimately had half-a-dozen of such accidents under their care.

Lord Campbell tried the case of the British Bank Directors, charged with the falsification of accounts and of various misrepresentations with a view to defraud the public; and although greatly assisted by the opening of Sir Frederick Thesiger, to which I have already alluded, it does not detract from the ability with which he mastered and dealt with its complicated details. His summing-up seemed to me to be conclusive of the guilt of all the defendants, although he recommended the jury to acquit one of them. They, however, were unable to realise any distinction between the different parties, and convicted them all; but whilst inflicting different terms of imprisonment upon the others, Lord Campbell did not punish the defendant in whose favour he had summed up. Speaking of this incident in his Diary, he says, ' I let one of them off with a nominal fine because he was improperly convicted.'

This was a very high-handed proceeding, and was severely commented upon, and motives not of a creditable character were suggested. I do not know whether there was, or not, any foundation for them, and therefore forbear to repeat them. The jury had throughout exhibited great intelligence, for which, before the verdict, they were highly complimented by the judge. I confess that it struck me that if this gentleman were entitled to be let off, the punishment of his companions could scarcely be deemed an act of justice.

I shall have again to refer to Lord Campbell in his position of head of Serjeants' Inn. The last time I saw him was on the afternoon of the day preceding his death. He was then Chancellor, and had, I believe, been presiding in the Court of Chancery. He was walking sturdily towards his own residence, in apparently perfect health and vigour, and, although he had attained an advanced age, the news of his death occasioned universal astonishment. I had not heard that he had exhibited any failure of power or diminution of intellect in the performance of his onerous duties, and certainly to the last he exhibited his untiring industry.

He was, to my great satisfaction, succeeded by Sir Richard Bethell, from whom I had already received many marks of kindness, and it was by his direction (he being Attorney-General) that I had been appointed one of the counsel to conduct the prosecution of the British Bank Directors ; and it was from him also that I afterwards obtained what I venture to think was a bare act of justice—a patent of precedence.

CHAPTER XVII.

I BECOME A SERJEANT.

As this chapter will, I fear, to ordinary readers be very dull, I have postponed it beyond many of the incidents that I have already related ; but as it refers to one of the most important events in my career, I must entreat their consideration and patience. I became a serjeant. The term is one that with the general public is surrounded with a sort of mysterious haze. Everyone knows what a sergeant is in the body militant ; and a sergeant of police is viewed by the masses with mingled feelings of terror and respect. We all know that the one is dressed in red, the other in blue. But what is a serjeant-at-law ? that is the question. Once, after I had attained this rank, I was counsel before a court-martial at Aldershot, and most hospitably invited to dinner at the mess —I think it was of the Welsh Fusiliers. When I presented myself and announced my name and title to the orderly, he informed me, with a scornful air, that it was an officers' mess. As a matter of

fact, we are only inferior in rank to a knight; and
formerly the position was a most important one, all
the great judicial offices being filled from its ranks,
and many a distinguished name is recorded in its
annals. The Queen's ancient serjeant, the head of
the body, was the foremost man at the bar. It
was not until the reign of Elizabeth that Queen's
Counsel were heard of; that arbitrary lady created
the first in the person of Francis Bacon. These
possess, however, no distinctive rank in society, but
simply precedence in court. The serjeants were,
and still are, joined in the commission with the
judges going circuit, which, until a comparatively
recent date, was not the case with Queen's Counsel.
Formerly they had exclusive audience in the Court
of Common Pleas; this is now abolished, and no
fault can reasonably be found with doing away with
a restriction injurious to clients and scarcely just
to the rest of the bar. Upon the abolition of this
privilege, the existing members of the court were
placed upon a level with the Queen's Counsel in
court by the grant of a patent of precedence.

I have already alluded to what I considered a
great grievance that I was subjected to by the
refusal of Lord Chelmsford to grant me this rank.
It had, subsequently to the opening of the court,
been granted to members of our body, and it could
not be asserted that my business was not such as

justified my application. Lord Campbell·also passed
me over, as he did Mr. Serjeant Parry, who had
an equal claim, although he gave it to Mr. Serjeant
Hayes, by which gentleman he sent a message that
my claim should be considered on a future occasion.
His death intervened, and I obtained the dignity
from Lord Westbury, but not before the delay had
been a considerable source of inconvenience to me,
if not of injury.

I do not propose giving any elaborate account
of the institution. My friend Serjeant Pulling has
done so in a very able article in the ' Edinburgh
Review.' [1] There was, however, one distinction between their rank and that of Queen's Counsel that
ought to be mentioned—the latter could not hold
a brief against the Crown without a licence ; the
coif was essentially a popular institution, and no
such restriction existed. It is true that the permission may be obtained, and the value set by her
Majesty upon her counsel being, I believe, 1l. 5s. 6d.,
he can for that price obtain permission to serve the
enemies of the State. This facility did not always
exist, and I believe that the difficulty occasioned the
employment of Mr. Serjeant Copley in the defence
of Dr. Watson, the circumstances attending which
I have already related. I cannot help thinking
that it is a great pity that the order should have

[1] The date of this extremely able and interesting article is Novem-
ber 1877.

been practically abolished, which however is the case, although legally it still exists. The result has arisen from the discountenance shown to it by later chancellors, their inconsistency with regard to patents, and ultimately by the necessity for judges taking the rank which formerly they were obliged to do being abolished.

I became serjeant in 1856, having been recommended by Sir John Jervis and created by Lord Cranworth, and I was duly elected to the Inn attached to the society.

The Lord Chief Justice (then Lord Campbell) presided, and the business of the Inn was conducted by a treasurer, a post filled at that time by Mr. Serjeant Manning, Queen's ancient serjeant. In the biography, recently published, Lord Campbell has recorded his opinion of his brethren upon the bench and of the serjeants. He had dined there only twice, but does not allow any want of self-confidence to interfere with the candour of his views. His words are : ' My brethren of the bench are a most respectable set. I believe them to be superior to their predecessors who filled their places fifty years ago.'

It would occupy too much space to describe the different most learned and able judges who formed the subject of this commendation, but by

some process of self-exaltation Lord Campbell
upon more occasions than this has apparently
assumed that the puisnés were a kind of inferior
beings to himself.   Amongst the names that occur
to me are those of Mr. Justice Coleridge and Mr.
Justice Erle, afterwards Chief Justice of the Court
of Common Pleas, both judges in the court over
which Lord Campbell presided, and Mr. Justice
Maule. The first-named, a most justly distinguished
judge, had retired before I had obtained much civil
business, and I can only therefore speak of his conduct of this branch of the profession from hearsay,
but I have always understood that he was a very
learned lawyer, and had great confidence reposed in
him by the profession and the public.   I can, however, speak of him as having been counsel before him
in many criminal trials, and I have no hesitation in
saying that no judge ever presided with greater
dignity, patience, and courtesy ; and if Lord Campbell had taken an example from him, he would
certainly have given more satisfaction, both as a
judge and a gentleman.   I may here venture to
record a very trifling circumstance which exhibited,
as I then thought and still think, great kindness of
heart.   In my early days I managed my voice very
badly, and was accustomed to strain it too much,
and having a case before him at the Kingston
assizes, Mr. Justice Coleridge sent me down a note

conveying a hint to me to avoid doing so, couched in very kind words.[1]

Of Mr. Justice Erle I shall speak hereafter, having seen more of him than of many of the other judges. I have had, however, many opportunities of forming an opinion of Mr. Justice Maule. I was very well acquainted with him, for in addition to practising before him we were members of the same club, the Union. He was one of Lord Campbell's respectable set, and certainly did not extend to the Lord Chief Justice even the modicum of praise accorded by that learned judge to himself. He entertained and constantly expressed for him the greatest contempt, and there is no doubt that Mr. Justice Maule did possess a much higher and nobler class of intellect. I used very often to dine with him, and was amazed at the variety of his knowledge, his acute grasp, and great reasoning powers. I have heard Sir John Jervis, who was chief of the court in which Maule sat, express quite as warm an opinion as I have done about his intellect. He was admitted to be a first-rate lawyer, and had been senior wrangler and senior medallist at Cambridge.

His manner was cynical, but he possessed a kind and humane disposition. He abhorred cruelty, and punished it with severity; but wherever he

---

[1] The last time I saw this learned judge was upon the Tichborne trial, when he had the satisfaction of seeing his son filling the office of Solicitor-General.

could find excuses in the natural failings of human nature, he always treated them with mercy. His jokes upon the bench were sometimes wanting in dignity, which laid him open to unfavourable comment. On one occasion a savage onslaught had been made upon him by Albany Fonblanque, the editor of the 'Examiner.' When told of it by some kind friend, he merely said, ' Well, I can't understand it, I never did him a favour.' Many good sayings are recorded of him, but they are more adapted to professional than general readers. He suffered dreadfully from asthma, and resigned his appointment after a paroxysm from which he suffered whilst sitting in the House of Lords.

The serjeants escaped the negative praise accorded to the judges. They were deemed by Lord Campbell to be entitled to something more positive, and his description of them is short and pithy. ' The serjeants,' says he, ' are a very degenerate race.' At the time this good-natured and charitable description was written I had not become a member of the body, but I should have been very happy to have shared their company. They were generally well-educated gentlemen, with an average of ability equal to any of the same number of members of the bar ; and, amongst them, there were those entitled upon many grounds to claim professional distinction. Mr. Serjeant Manning, the treasurer, was a very learned and distinguished lawyer, well versed in black-letter writings, and his opinions upon such subjects were esteemed of great value.   I can thoroughly well understand the contempt that Lord Campbell entertained for him, as he never knew how to turn his knowledge into profit. I cannot, however, but smile at the recollection of him.   He was old himself when I joined the Inn, and ably represented its antiquity.   He was very strict in making us eat and drink after the manner of our ancestors; any relaxation gave him serious disturbance, and I am afraid that my want of reverence caused him no small amount of heart-burning; but after all, his foibles were innocent enough, and might have been recorded by a kindly pen.   Another degenerate was Mr. Serjeant Storks.   To be sure, he was a gentleman and a wit.   He was a good lawyer also, and led the Norfolk Circuit.   It was no disgrace to him that a more powerful man, Sir Fitzroy Kelly, was too much for his calibre.   When I first knew him, his powers were somewhat impaired by age.   He was a great admirer of men whom he called the giants.   Lord Ellenborough was his idol. Of Lord Campbell he used to say that he had got on as much by trickery as by real merit, and that he was the greatest jobber that had ever flourished at the bar.   As one instance of his accomplishment in this capacity, Storks used to relate, that in his reports Campbell, for the first time, published the names of the attorneys in the various cases, which he found led to useful introductions. If degenerate himself, Serjeant Storks had the good fortune to be father of General Storks, the well-known and distinguished officer. Mr. Serjeant Hayes came within his lordship's list. He also possessed the qualities that probably entitled him to the description at Lord Campbell's hands, for he was a thorough gentleman, an accomplished lawyer, and a kind friend, but never succeeded in making a large income. As long as he remained amongst the degenerates, he was the soul of the table. He was a leader upon the Midland Circuit, at the mess of which his conversational powers added greatly to the enjoyment of the members, and his kindness of disposition endeared him to every one.

Lord Campbell himself, pitying his degeneracy, raised him to the ranks of respectability, in which atmosphere, however, he did not long survive.[1]

Mr. Serjeant Shee, another gentleman coming within Lord Campbell's category, was a Roman Catholic. He led with great power and success the Maidstone sessions, and, subsequently taking the coif, obtained a considerable lead upon the Home

[1] He was created a Judge of the Queen's Bench and died suddenly at the Court.

Circuit. He was a very able speaker, but somewhat heavy. He was certainly a scholar and a high-
minded gentleman, but not having met with great
success was entitled to the sneers of Lord Campbell.
He too became a judge, but did not enjoy his promotion for any great length of time. He was greatly
liked at Serjeants' Inn, and would have been respected in any association where gentlemen and
lawyers met. He it was who defended Palmer in the
case of which already I have given some account.

One more degenerate, Mr. Serjeant Pigott, became eminent as a Baron of the Exchequer. He
was a contemporary of Baron Huddleston, both of
them being called upon the same day, and both of
them leaders of the Oxford Circuit. He was much
liked, and, if not a powerful man, was a thoroughly
conscientious judge.

Upon Mr. Serjeant Manning's retirement, Mr.
Serjeant Gazelee became treasurer of the Inn.
This gentleman was the son of a judge. His father
has been delivered to posterity as having presided
at the famous trial of Bardell v. Pickwick. I just
remember him, and certainly he was deaf. I believe him to have been a learned lawyer. His
son was a man of good ability, and had the advantage of a college education and first-rate introductions. He was not troubled with much diffidence,
nor did he extend extravagant praise to his fellow-

creatures ; but as far as I know he never be-
haved with unkindness, and I have heard of many
generous and disinterested acts that he has performed.   He was succeeded, I believe not immediately, by Mr. Serjeant Tozer in the office of
treasurer.

In the year 1872, upon his resignation, I was
elected in his place.   I found that for some time
past the expenditure had been excessive, and that
many gross abuses had gradually crept in.   I
dismissed most of the servants, and made many
alterations.   I found that better entertainment
could be supplied at a cheaper rate, and I remember with much satisfaction the cordial way
in which I was supported by the judges and my
brother serjeants.   Our little dinners in the hall,
formerly a chapel, on the windows of which were
emblazoned the arms of many old and distinguished
members of the Inn, and upon whose walls hung the
pictures of eminent lawyers, were marked by good
temper and friendly feeling.   I was elected annually
until the year 1875, when I accepted a retainer to go
to India, and sent in my resignation, and my friend
Mr. Serjeant Simon was elected in my place, but
upon my return that gentleman resigned, and, being
reinstated, I remained treasurer until the abolition of the Inn ; and now, although its duties are
abolished, and its convivialities are no more, the

order still exists, and, if I have no other word inscribed on the roll of fame, I shall be recorded as the last treasurer of one of the most ancient, and at one time the most honoured, of the institutions of Great Britain. As the order was virtually abolished, it was determined to sell the property of the Inn, which was accordingly done, and the last meeting was held on April 27, 1877, when the resolution recorded below was come to.

Present—Lord Chief Justice Cockburn ; Lord Chief Justice Coleridge ; Lord Chief Baron Kelly ; Mr. Baron Bramwell ; Mr. Justice Brett ; Sir Montague Smith ; Mr. Justice Mellor ; Mr. Justice Lush ; Mr. Justice Denman ; Mr. Justice Grove ; Mr. Baron Pollock ; Mr. Baron Huddleston ; Mr. Justice Lindley ; Serjeant Parry ; Serjeant Simon ; Serjeant Wells ; Serjeant Petersdorff ; Serjeant Pulling.

It was proposed by the Lord Chief Justice, and seconded by the Lord Chief Baron, and carried unanimously, 'That the cordial thanks of this meeting, on behalf of all the members of the society, be given to Mr. Serjeant Ballantine for his long and valuable services as the Treasurer of Serjeants' Inn, and that he be requested to select from the property of the society such a piece of plate as he may think proper as a substantial memento of the good feeling towards him of the members of the society.'

It would be very ungenerous on my part if I did not acknowledge my obligations to Mr. Serjeant Pulling, whose industry and research had much to do with the successful arrangements that were made, and who also received a piece of plate. Three of my brethren have passed away, Serjeant Parry, Serjeant O'Brien, and Serjeant Sargood, all men of ability. The first attained great distinction, Serjeant O'Brien not as much as his talents deserved, and Serjeant Sargood was one of the ablest of the advocates in parliamentary business ; and, although my meetings with the remainder are now, I am sorry to say, but rare, my feelings of respect and affection for them are undiminished.

When I joined Serjeants' Inn I was compelled to leave the Inner Temple, into which society I have since been received back, and also am generously permitted to enjoy the hospitality of the bench table as an honorary member.

CHAPTER XVIII.

THE GARRICK CLUB.

AGAIN in defiance of chronology, I am about to go
back many years and describe another institution.
I could wish that an abler pen than mine would
perform the task, nevertheless it is a labour of love
—my theme is the old Garrick Club, then occupying
a small, unpretending-looking house in King Street,
Covent Garden. There was, however, no resort in
London that could boast of attracting so much of
brilliancy and wit.

Named after Garrick, it was naturally sought
by actors, poets, artists, and novelists, and members
of the graver professions were only too glad to
relieve the labours of the day by the society of
all that was distinguished in literature and art.
Although I joined it early in my career, I was
not an original member, and missed those convivial meetings that I have heard described, in
which Theodore Hook, Barham, and the brothers Smith[1] shone and sparkled with so brilliant
a light; and when the memory dwells upon

[1] Authors of the 'Rejected Addresses.'

'Gilbert Gurney,' the 'Ingoldsby Legends,' and 'Rejected Addresses,' I can imagine at times, when their authors met in the social smoking-room, there must have been an absolute surfeit of fun. Of Theodore Hook I am well able to judge, having, as I have already related, frequently met him. I also knew Barham. He used to dine with a friend of mine named Walsh, delighting the guests with his refined humour. The Smiths I never have had the pleasure of meeting. But I must not gibbet myself as a 'laudator temporis acti,' for, although a new generation had sprung up when I joined the club, it was by no means an undistinguished one. Dickens and Thackeray had made their marks, and they were broad and lasting ones. But of these writers I have already recorded my impressions.

Stansfield and David Roberts were noble representatives of art. The former, the great painter of ocean beauty and grandeur, was not often at the club, and I can scarcely recall his appearance. But David was there constantly, when his kindly, good-humoured face, reminding one of a country farmer upon market day, would often expand itself at our pleasant gatherings. I do not think that a greater favourite existed in the club. Charles Kemble was frequently there, but, alas! no one could have recognised in his appearance the gentlemanlike swagger with which once upon a time he portrayed 'The Inconstant,' or the mixture of fun, dignity, and embarrassment he had been wont to convey in 'The Merry Monarch.' If any of my readers would like to obtain an idea of this charming actor during his best days, there is an excellent picture of him in a scene with Fawcett and Maria Tree, in which he portrays Charles II. It hangs upon the walls of the club : he was then the embodiment of life, but the light of those days had departed, he had become very deaf, and, like many people suffering from that infirmity, used every endeavour to make himself hear. This was impossible, but others were fully informed of his thoughts ; and as these were occasionally far from complimentary to the hearer, his presence latterly in the club was looked upon with some apprehension.

Charles Kean was a most worthy representative of the drama. He, it is well known, was the son of one of the greatest and most original actors that ever lived. He was highly educated, and his tastes and feelings were refined. He set an example of most careful and laborious study, and, whether in a particular piece he attained success or not, he never spared time or pains to deserve it. There were some parts in which he was very successful. I think that his best effort was in ' Louis XI.,' a play translated from the French. If he were alive, however, I would not venture to say that he excelled in melo-drama, and certainly did not in Shakespeare. In the 'Corsican Brothers' he was admirable, and in a translation of Carré's 'Faust,' in which he played Me-phistopheles, I never saw any better performance.

Upon its first night he deviated from the strict propriety that ordinarily characterised everything he did by offering to bet two to one in bishops; but it being suggested that this would indicate a superfluity of such articles in his dominions, he excised it from his part.   He was the most sensitive man I ever knew in my life.   A great feud existed between him and Albert Smith.   The original cause I forget, but he had offended Albert, who put into some penny paper that a patient audience had en-dured the infliction of Charles Kean in 'Hamlet' in the expectation of seeing the Keeleys in the after-piece.   One night I and a member named Arabin, the son of Mr. Serjeant Arabin, were talking with Albert Smith in the coffee-room.   At the opposite side stood Charles Kean, scowling.   Presently Albert departed.   In about three strides Charles Kean reached us.   'Richard,' he said, in the most tragic of voices, 'I never thought that you, my old school-fellow, would have consorted with that viper.' Poor good-natured Dick had heard nothing of the quar-rel.   On another occasion it is related that he ad-dressed an old orange woman at his theatre whom he had discovered applauding Ryder,[1] who had been playing in the same piece with himself, in something of these terms, ' Ungrateful wretch ! thou who hast eaten of my bread and enjoyed the hospitality of my roof, how couldest thou applaud that man?' But, after all, these were but foibles, and he was in all substantial respects a credit to his profession.

I have already spoken of that little round object with a bald head and fresh-coloured face, and somewhat serious expression of countenance, no longer almost a supernumerary, but now the very funniest of comedians, not trusting to grins and distortions, but thoroughly artistic in his comedy, Robert Keeley. There are many now upon the stage of equal ability, but none with the same characteristics. There are some, but they are still alive, whose names I ought next to record, but as I am down amongst the dead men, and my living friends will feel no jealousy about precedence, let me mention poor Leigh Murray. What a promising actor he was, and how much courted ! It was unlucky for his future fame that he was so. He followed pleasure, and sacrificed life. Albert and Arthur Smith—how sad to be obliged to class them in the death-category ! Their addresses had not been rejected, but their enjoyment of their success was only too short. Albert married the eldest daughter

---

[1] This gentleman was a member of Charles Kean's company at the Princess's, and is still a well-known actor.

of Keeley, and she very soon followed him to the grave. There were plenty of lawyers, some still alive, but many of them have passed away.

Ought I to say more than I have already done of Serjeant Talfourd—as genial in the club as in his own house, and qualified as member in every capacity that formed a claim for entering it? Another serjeant was there also ; he was not great, nor did he possess literary powers, but he was connected with the editor of ' Bell's Life,' who was, I believe, his brother. His name was Dowling, and he was once, when a junior, in a cause with Gurney as his leader. A witness had been called and told to go down. ' Allow me to ask a question,' said Dowling. ' Certainly,' said Gurney, who would have snapped his head off if he had not been allied to a newspaper. He asked one single question. In the next Sunday paper a paragraph in the following words appeared: ' Here Mr. Dowling rose and, with a most impressive tone and manner, asked the witness where he lived.' Yet another let me mention of those who are no more—kindly, genial, good-natured Morgan John O'Connell. He was contented with his illustrious name, being nephew of the Liberator, and did not seek to add to its laurels ; but everywhere he was a favourite. We witnessed together a most appalling incident ; it will never pass from my memory. We were seated one night at the club, when the whole sky became lighted up, and it was apparent that a large fire was raging. We started off in search of it, and found that it had broken out upon some warehouses situated upon the south-east side of London Bridge. They had contained an immense quantity of oil, which escaped in a state of ignition and spread itself over the surface of the river, presenting to the eyes of a beholder a sea of flame. Some unhappy creatures in a boat approaching too near were sucked into the fiery gulf. We heard one horrible shriek as if coming from a single voice, we witnessed arms struggling in unspeakable agony, and then the pitiless element closed over them for ever. No picture of pandemonium has ever equalled the horror of this frightful reality. It haunted me for weeks.

From a sad scene, where could my thoughts more pleasantly wander than to Shirley Brooks and my friend and brother Serjeant Parry, who was one of the most popular of the lawyers belonging to the club; and, although not a member, I have often met Douglas Jerrold there, the very bitterest of satirists and most epigrammatic of authors. Of Albert Smith I have already spoken. And let me end my obituary—how sad to think how long it is! —with one celebrity, by no means the least valued or appreciated. He was almost an institution in himself, and pity it is that he was only mortal : it was Mr. Hamblet. He called himself the steward of the club, but this was only the modesty of a great man. He was its dictator, and reigned supreme. The sense of his position sat in placid dignity upon his countenance, as he moved about extending an occasional recognition to a favourite member. Sometimes, if he discovered any breach of the rules, a single frown upon his face made the culprit shrink abashed. For many years he ruled, and there were no rebels to his authority ; but at last he also yielded to the decrees of fate, and his like will ne'er be seen again.

It seemed only proper that, after he had passed away, the old house should not long survive, and now the members of the Garrick occupy a handsome edifice in a street named after it. Some of its rooms are very good, the drawing-room and the smoking-room particularly so : in the former, the fine pictures of its excellent collection are very advantageously seen ; and in the latter, there are upon the walls paintings presented by Stansfield and Roberts, and some interesting ones by an artist of the name, I believe, of Haig. I doubt, however, whether the club is so cosy as it was ; although there are still members in it whom I knew in early days, and who will, I trust, long keep out of my former list.

The stage could not be better or more honourably represented than by the veteran Walter Lacey, a sterling actor, always ready to do his very utmost to please, both in public and private ; excellent in some parts, and far above mediocrity in all he has attempted. I have known him well throughout the greater part of his career. Then there is my old friend Palgrave Simpson, accomplished as a writer, and almost unrivalled as an amateur actor. But what business have I to call him old ? He is as young as ever, and would have been without a rival were it not for Tom Holmes, to whom every accomplishment seemed to come by nature. History gives him many years of life, his appearance and talents much fewer. His last performance was in an amateur pantomime, where he delighted an immense audience, including royalty, by a wonderfully active and witty performance of pantaloon.

Of course in recording old reminiscences it would be impossible to forget Frank Fladgate, now, I believe, the father of the club, and who, for all the years it has existed, and through all its changing scenes, has never made an enemy. No one of the present day is so conversant with the records of the stage and the lives of the greatest actors; and it is a real treat to listen to his pleasant talk, and note his adoration of his beloved Shakespeare.

One other of my oldest friends I must mention, and then adieu to the old Garrick. Not only in this club did I know Isadore Brasseur, but we were brother members of the Clarence, and we frequently met amongst mutual friends. He had been a professor at King's College, and in that capacity became known to the Prince of Wales, who has ever since exhibited towards him the most cordial affection. We do not now often see him amongst us; but there are no lack of English friends who are glad to seek ' Le Chevalier Brasseur ' in his pleasant Paris home.

And now *vale valete*. It would be an agreeable task to refer to other living members distinguished in literature, in art, in the drama, in the army, and in my own profession ; but the catalogue would be too long, and so I have confined myself to a word or two about those only whom, dead or living, I have known and valued in the early days of the old club-house, and the estimation in which it is now held could not be better testified than that it boasts amongst its members His Royal Highness the Prince of Wales.

CHAPTER XIX.

INEQUALITY OF SENTENCES

A REFLECTION that forces itself upon the mind of every one who has observed the machinery of our courts is how very much the fate of men and causes must depend upon the temper and disposition of those who preside ; there is such an enormous amount of discretion vested in judges, which might be limited, although it could not be abolished. I do not believe that a code could be so formed as to meet the multifarious requirements of our complicated state of existence : but I do think that in certain matters grave scandals are created by the apparent inequality of decisions, and I think it would look better in the eyes of the public and be much more satisfactory for the judge if a certain sentence always followed the same verdict, and mitigating circumstances were left for the executive to deal with. This subject is a very large one, and it is not upon any assumption that I am capable of dealing with it that I have made the allusion I have done ; but it has arisen from thinking how very

different in every mental feature was Sir Frederick
Pollock, who became Chief Baron of the Exchequer
after the death of Lord Abinger, from his contemporary, Lord Campbell. I remember the former,
from the earliest period of my life, as Mr. Frederick
Pollock. He lived opposite to our house in Serjeants' Inn. His elder brother David practised in
the old Insolvent Court in Portugal Street, where
my father also endeavoured to obtain business.
Pollock was at one time member for Huntingdon,
and Somersham, my mother's birthplace, being in
the same county, as he rose in the profession he
was a man of mark in the eyes of my family. It
also so happened that in very early days I possessed
a client and friend, Frank Betham, who entrusted
him with his business, and occasionally gave me the
junior briefs of which I have already recorded one
instance. When franks were in use I was proud to
obtain Pollock's signature. I have watched him in
and out of office, and no one had more vicissitudes.
A banker of Huntingdon named Veasey was his
intimate friend. This gentleman occupied a house
that once belonged to my mother in that town, and
he also belonged to the Union Club, where I often
heard him repeat the praises of Sir Frederick, who
received the appointment of Chief Baron whilst
conducting a case at the Central Court of which
hereafter I have given an account, and I hope

that I shall not detract from his dignity by saying that he did not conceal his delight. I look back to him with much affectionate regard, which may possibly bias my opinion; but I am not afraid to assert that no stain ever found its way upon his escutcheon, and no charge of jobbery ever followed his well-deserved success. He was in fact an upright and honourable gentleman. His attainments were of a very high order. He took the first honours at Cambridge, and almost down to his death took delight in the most abstruse problems in mathematics. He belonged to a race of lawyers to whom the latest hours of night and the earliest in the morning presented no impediment to study, and almost to the last he was fond of putting upon his letters the very early hour at which they were written. I am not quite sure that I must not attribute to him some small share of personal vanity, as he was accustomed to sit upon the bench nursing a very handsome leg and foot, and looking at it with great complacency. One of his numerous daughters was married to Mr., afterwards Baron, Martin, and the active, energetic, and powerful mind of this gentleman possessed great weight with his father-in-law, and gave rise to some comments which certainly, as far as intentions went, were not deserved.

There is always great difficulty in avoiding

criticism, however honest may be the endeavour, when a successful advocate practises before a near connection. It has been my lot to be engaged before him in many cases. He possessed firmness and decision, and though sometimes hasty, he was never harsh or discourteous. I do not think a young counsel ever had to complain of injustice being done to him, and he thoroughly appreciated merit. Although solemn in his manner, both upon the bench and in society, I have heard him make the best after-dinner speech that I ever listened to, except from the lips of Dickens. Amongst the *causes célèbres* that were tried before him was that of the Mannings, for a very brutal murder in Bermondsey. It excited much attention at the time, Mrs. Manning having been maid to a lady of distinguished rank, and having subsequently followed a career that made her somewhat generally known. I defended her unsuccessfully, as she was hanged; and, although she was my client, I suspect she was the power that really effected the deed.

I was once counsel in the Court of Exchequer in a curious and interesting case. It was an action brought by executors against a life insurance company to recover the amount of a sum insured upon the life of a person who, it was alleged, was accidentally drowned. It appeared that shortly after the insurance had been effected he went down to Brighton, and stated to the people at the house where he put up that he was going out to bathe, and his clothes were found upon the beach, but he himself did not return. His relatives claimed the amount of the insurance money. The company disputed the claim. Some little time after the disappearance, a body, in a partial state of decomposition, was cast on shore on one of the Channel islands. The parties interested did not feel the least difficulty in identifying the body as that of their lost relative, but, on the other hand, there were no natural means by which it could have got from Brighton to the coast where it was found. Several witnesses were called upon this point, and I remember making the Chief Baron laugh by a very indifferent joke. A doctor had been examined, and some little delay occurred. My lord got impatient, and said, somewhat pettishly, ' Who is your next witness, brother ? ' ' Well, my lord,' I answered, ' having called the doctor, the next in order will be the undertaker.'

The jury were ultimately discharged, and the claim was never renewed. Of its fraudulent nature there is not the smallest doubt. It was shown that in all cases of drowning at Brighton the body was cast back if the immersion had taken place near the shore, and the currents made it simply impossible that it could reach the spot where the body identified was cast. Sir Frederick had a very retentive memory for faces, and on one occasion that he was trying a case a little attorney named Cyrus Jay was a witness. This gentleman, one &c., was not known in the higher professional walks, and I fancy entered the witness-box with some trepidation. The chief, however, as was his habit, and is the habit of all experienced judges, scanned Cyrus very attentively, and, having heard his name, said, 'Are you any relation of my old friend Dr. Jay of Bristol?' 'I am his son,' said the witness. In subsequently telling this anecdote, Cyrus added, 'After that I felt I could swear anything I liked.' In the case I am about to record I think that Sir Frederick Pollock laid down the law wrongly; in the way, however, he directed the jury the verdict returned was the only one open for them to give; but the history of it, for many reasons that I shall mention, is worth recording. It was an action against the Great Eastern Railway Company by a gentleman who undoubtedly had been seriously injured in an accident upon that line, and which had been occasioned by the fracture of the tire of one of the wheels of the engine.

Now whether such a fracture could have been prevented by reasonable care is a question of great difficulty, and can only be determined by the evidence of engineers. These gentlemen have

undergone an apprenticeship before committees
of the House of Commons, and have learnt to give
plausible reasons for all the propositions they advance, and as counsel can rarely shake them, he
had better leave them alone, trusting to the same
number of witnesses he is instructed to call on the
other side. It is then that Greek meets Greek.
Engineers have more power, for the above reason,
when in a witness-box, than other professional witnesses. The inside also of a bar of iron is more of
a *terra incognita* than even the inside of a human
body; at all events there are fewer people who
know anything about it; but medical men who do
not make a trade of being witnesses are frequently
much embarrassed when called upon to give
reasons for their opinions. They are accustomed
to rule supreme in the sick chamber, and their
judgment is not disputed. Very likely they are
right in their evidence, but are not the less embarrassed. I doubt much whether a parson who had
preached the soundest of doctrine would be able to
uphold it in the teeth of a rigorous cross-examination. I have been engaged in many cases involving
mechanical and medical questions. In the former
I have trusted to members of the same profession; in the latter, generally to myself. In the
case in question no fault was to be found with the
wheel that had given way, but two most eminent

engineers, amongst the very highest in their profession, declared that they had seen the corresponding wheel, which had not been removed from a siding upon the railway where it had been taken to after the accident, and that they had examined it with great care, and had discovered in it a fissure into which they could easily have placed the blade of a knife. One of them said he had actually done so. As the company did not anticipate any evidence about this particular wheel, we were not prepared with engineers upon the other side, who might have treated the fissure as totally immaterial, and the Lord Chief Baron, as I think improperly, held that its existence was evidence of negligence. Perhaps it was, but surely not negligence affecting the accident. However, the jury found, as they were bound to do upon the ruling, a substantial verdict for the plaintiff, who had lost a leg.

Another person injured in the same accident brought an action against the company in the Court of Common Pleas, but in the interval the wheel alleged to be defective was exhumed and examined, and upon the trial it was produced, and it showed incontestably that there was not upon it either speck or blemish. An endeavour was made to discredit the fact that it was the same wheel, the engineers who had obtained the verdict in the Court of Exchequer reasserting and repeating their evidence. Thus it became a matter of fact and not of science, and Lord Chief Justice Cockburn, before whom the case was tried, so left it to the jury, and they, with scarcely a moment's hesitation, found for the defendants.

Whilst upon this subject, I may mention a case in which I was counsel for the same company, tried at Croydon before Chief Baron Kelly, and in which the tire of a wheel had given way, and much of the engineering talent of the country was called upon one side or the other. After a very long trial the company obtained a verdict. But the case is interesting principally from the evidence that was given in relation to the smelting of the iron previous to formation into bars, showing how an almost imperceptible grain of any foreign substance getting into the molten mass would create the nucleus of extensive injury, which, if not upon the surface, would be undiscoverable by any tests ; consequently that the accidents that happened to the tires usually occurred with perfectly new wheels, the old ones having had their capacities thoroughly tested.

Sir Frederick Pollock was very fond of the Home Circuit, and I have frequently had the opportunity of enjoying his great social qualities at Farnham Castle, the residence of the late Dr. Sumner, then Bishop of Winchester. It was a real relaxation to

go from Guildford to this very beautiful spot, where
the prelate extended to the bar the most liberal
hospitality.   His   parties   were   rendered   more
agreeable   by   the   guests   from   Aldershot,   and
young and old, red coats and black, met with the
most cheery welcome, greatly enhanced by the accomplishments and courtesy of the ladies of the
family.

The bishop was very fond of his garden, and
with him, and enjoying his simple thoughts and
polished. conversation, and sharing, as I did, his
love for birds and flowers, I have passed many an
hour that in a circuit town would have hung
heavily enough.   I have already mentioned David
Pollock.   He went out to Bombay as chief justice,
and there died.   Another brother, as is well known,
was a most distinguished general, and received the
thanks of his country for the services he performed.
Sir Frederick retired from the Bench, receiving the
honour of a baronetcy, and making way for Sir
Fitzroy Kelly.   He was a consistent Tory, and
passed through the different changes that the party
underwent, and when at last he came to the front
I fancy there were very few in the profession that
grudged him his good fortune.

It is not a bad story that is told of him when
upon the Northern Circuit.   A gentleman named
Alexander had a large leading practice, and it was

noticed that Mr. Pollock, as he then was, always made complimentary allusions to him. Some one asked him how he could possibly do so. 'Why,' said he, 'do you not perceive that if I did not keep Alexander in business, I should have that fellow Cresswell against me in every case?'

When the Guildford assizes, the last place of the summer circuit, ended, I seldom lost much time in hastening abroad, and my steps seemed naturally to turn to Boulogne-sur-Mer. I was very fond of the place. It is now a good deal changed. The abolition of imprisonment for debt has enabled most of the unwilling sojourners to return to their native shores, and thus it has lost the gayest and most careless of its residents. At the time I am now recalling, most of them belonged to a little club, held in the Rue de l'Ecu. Taken generally, their original social rank was good, and their manners were easy and gentlemanlike. We played whist at franc points, and I need not say that no credit was asked for or given. One or other of the members would disappear for a time. It was understood that he was putting up at the 'English hotel,' by which name the debtors' prison was designated. If any of us were fortunate enough to have a run of luck, and win some five pounds or so, the club was deserted by the whist-players during the week following, whilst the lucky winner might be seen, probably for the only time that season, enjoying his dinner and Lafitte at one of the best *tables d'hôte*. One of the characters I remember was an Irish major, a thorough good specimen of his country. He was a tolerably regular frequenter of the whist-table, and played an excellent rubber. He had a son, an officer of high distinction in the Indian army. Very precise was the major in his demeanour, and careful in his play. From the few words that occasionally escaped his lips, and from what was heard of him from other quarters, it was clear that he had moved in the higher circles, and had at one time been possessed of large means; but he never either boasted or complained. We learned that after a short illness he had died in a solitary lodging, and also a sad tale of the poverty that surrounded him. The circumstances which existed in India at that period prevented his son from knowing anything of his position. When his desk was opened, a number of memoranda were found, showing that, however polished his associates may have been, they did not possess much honesty; and there were signatures of some well-known persons to I O U's who might, if they had paid a tenth of what they owed him, have enabled him to live and die in comfort.

Should the above lines meet the eyes of his son,

I trust he will not feel that I have improperly
drawn aside a curtain that ought to have been
kept closed, but it has been done in no unkindly
spirit.

Amongst the figures that were not gay or
thoughtless, I well remember Alderman Kennedy,
who was one of those convicted upon the British
Bank trial, and upon whose face and in whose
weary footstep the observer would discover hopeless despondency. Vanity had been his ruin.
He had by most honourable means realised a large
fortune in India, and he believed that he was equal
to cope with the intrigue and trickery of the rascals
of this metropolis. By his connection with the
British Bank he sacrificed fortune and character.

I knew him very well before his fall, a weak,
pompous, kindly hearted man. He could not see
any element in nature superior to himself. Oh,
how wearily he trod those stones! I sought to
renew my acquaintance with him, but he rejected
all my overtures. Poor fellow, sinned against, but
having in truth no fraud in his own thoughts, he
died in a foreign place, and the epitaph upon his
tomb ought to have been—Victim of self-conceit.

Charles Dickens was very fond of Boulogne,
and on the occasion that I particularly remember
him in the place, he occupied a villa upon the
Calais road. Albert and Arthur Smith were also

frequent visitors. They used to catch little fish in the harbour, as in former days they did in the lake of Geneva. And I also met an old acquaintance of mine, an eminent physician, Dr. Elliotson. He carried on his profession in Conduit Street, Regent Street, and had formerly enjoyed a very large practice; but he became a convert to mesmerism, which he fancied could be made a valuable agent in the treatment of disease. Unless a reformer can crush, he must be crushed, and Elliotson being an enthusiast and not an impostor, the holy war of etiquette was waged by his profession against him and ruined his business.

Upon one occasion this gentleman, Charles Dickens, and myself started together in the packet from Boulogne for Folkestone. Neither of my comrades was a good sailor, and they knew it themselves. The illustrious author armed himself with a box of homœopathic globules; and the doctor, whose figure was rotund, having a theory that by tightening the stomach the internal movements which caused the sickness might be prevented, waddled down to the boat with his body almost divided by a strap. The weather was stormy, and neither remedy proved of any avail.

I frequently met Dr. Elliotson in society. He was a man of very varied attainments, and a great favourite. Amongst the houses at which he was a constant visitor was that of a lady, Mrs. Milner Gibson, who at one time gathered around her a large circle, comprising most of those famous in literature, art, and the professions; and here also every foreigner possessing a grievance and an unhappy country was always made heartily welcome.

Dr. Elliotson was also a much valued guest at Mr. Justice Crowder's, where I used to meet him. This judge I remember with great feelings of pleasure, joined to regret at his comparatively early death.

He had been on the Western Circuit with Cockburn, and, being his senior in the House of Commons, might have contested with him the honour of the Solicitor-Generalship; but he preferred the safer and easier position of a seat on the Bench, which he filled with general respect and approval.

CHAPTER XX.

MURDER OF MR. DRUMMOND.

In the commencement of the year 1843, as a gentleman named Drummond was walking down Parliament Street, he was fatally wounded by a pistol-shot, fired by a man of the name of MacNaghten, a Scotchman. It was clear that he was mistaken by him for Sir Robert Peel, whom it was his intention to have killed. As Mr. Drummond was a man generally respected, and of the most inoffensive habits, it was not unnatural that a storm of indignation should arise against the perpetrator of the act, whilst the patience exhibited by his victim during the few days that he survived the attack added to the general sympathy of the public.

NacNaghten was placed upon his trial for murder in the following February, Sir Nicholas Conyngham Tindal, Chief Justice of the Common Pleas, presiding. I have had occasion to refer to this judge, although not at any length, when giving an account of the Courvoisier trial. He was certainly not a man of startling characteristics, but upon the bench presented a singularly calm and equable appearance. I never saw him yield to irritability, or exhibit impatience. I should say in fact that he was made for the position that he filled, and sound law and substantial justice were sure, as far as human power could prevail, to be administered under his presidency.

It required a judge of this calibre to control the violent feelings of indignation launched not unnaturally against the accused. Sir William Follett conducted the prosecution, and the late Lord Chief Justice, then Mr. Cockburn, was retained for the defence.

The facts were easily proved, and the only question that was in issue was whether the prisoner at the time of the commission of the crime was of sound mind, and the onus of showing the contrary practically devolved upon the prisoner's counsel.[1] MacNaghten had been treated as a lunatic, and he appears to have imagined that Sir Robert Peel was bent upon his destruction, which he intended to prevent by the assassination. There was no ground whatever for even the belief that Sir Robert Peel knew him.

In a case not altogether analogous, but bearing some similarity to it, Erskine had made a most

---

[1] This is not so theoretically, as the indictment in terms declares the accused to be of sound mind and understanding.

masterly and argumentative speech, dealing with
the different phases of insanity, and Cockburn in
his defence of MacNaghten had the advantage of
that great advocate's views and treatment of the
subject. This, however, did not detract from the
merit of one of the most masterly arguments ever
heard at the English bar. Several witnesses were
called, and the facts that I have briefly stated were
fully proved. Before the evidence was concluded,
the Chief Justice appealed to Sir William Follett,
who admitted that he must submit to a verdict acquitting the prisoner upon the ground of insanity,
and this verdict was accordingly pronounced. A
storm of indignation followed it. Mad or not, the
prisoner ought to have been hanged. Such was no
uncommon expression, and a general denunciation
of mad doctors, and some not very complimentary
remarks upon lawyers, might not unfrequently be
heard. This outcry resulted in a very singular proceeding on the part of the House of Lords, which
had no precedent, and fortunately has never been
repeated. The judges were summoned by their
lordships to express their opinions upon the law
applicable to insanity in criminal cases. It seems
to me surprising that they did not point out that
such a proceeding was extra-judicial, and that their
opinions could only properly be given upon certain
facts arising before them in their judicial capacity,

and that what was asked of them was to make a
law in anticipation of facts that might hereafter
arise. The same proceeding also might be adopted
in relation to any subject, civil or criminal. However, the judges went and sat in solemn conclave,
but as might be expected, being called upon to
found abstract opinions with no facts to go upon,
they have not greatly assisted the administration
of justice.[1]

The important points propounded by the judges
seem to be as follows :—

'The only ground upon which an alleged
lunatic is entitled to an acquittal is *that he did
not know the difference between right and wrong
in the act that he committed.*' If they had proceeded to say upon what principles this question
was to be determined, some benefit might have
arisen from their opinions.

The judges further say, ' that although a person
may in a particular matter act under an insane
delusion, and act in consequence thereof, he is
equally liable with a person of sane mind.' I
presume this to mean that unless it be shown that
the delusion destroyed his knowledge of the difference between right and wrong, which is to be
discovered and proved independently of the admitted delusion, he must be considered of sane

---

[1] Mr. Justice Maule pointed out this difficulty.

mind. If these dicta are to be received as law, then a totally different principle governs civil and criminal cases, and a person incapable of making a will or executing a deed may, nevertheless, be liable to be executed for the commission of what in a sane person would be a crime. However startling this proposition is, it cannot be controverted, and it appears to me that the subject is one worthy of further consideration and much more careful analysis than have ever been applied to it. In the observations that I have already made, and in those that follow, I do not pretend to lay down any proposition or dictate any solution of the difficulty, but merely wish to suggest certain matters that in the course of my practice have presented themselves to my mind with a view of attracting the attention of better-informed and more experienced men.

That insanity exists to a most deplorable extent is testified by the numerous establishments, both public and private, for the care of lunatics, and the question of how far mental derangement, admitted to exist upon a particular point, affects the conduct of an individual beyond the scope of that point, is a subject worthy of the research both of medical men and lawyers. Doctors have introduced the term 'uncontrollable impulse,' and an excuse has been sought under this term for violent bursts of passion arising from natural causes; but are not such symptoms also the result of insanity? Have we not numerous instances in which under such influences the victims have destroyed themselves? It is not difficult to presume that they knew they were doing wrong; and, indeed, the cunning that in many cases attends their acts indicates that they did; but assuming one of the qualities of the sane human mind to be self-restraint, and supposing this barrier has been removed by insanity, ought the sufferer to be held criminally liable for his acts, although evidence existed that he was conscious of the difference between right and wrong?

When Ravaillac assassinated Henry IV. of France, he believed that in doing so he was commending himself to God, and as many enthusiasts at all times and in all countries have acted under such impressions, it would be a dangerous doctrine to declare that because the sense of right and wrong had disappeared, a criminal should be deemed irresponsible; and yet, on the other hand, an utter lunatic may possess a sense of right and wrong in many actions of his life. The case is well known of a madman who was cross-examined by Erskine ineffectually for some time. At last the counsel obtained the clue, and in answer to a question he put the witness said, 'I am the Christ.' Upon a subsequent occasion, when again cross-examined, he carefully avoided the admission that had defeated him upon the former occasion. He was admittedly a lunatic, but certainly if he had been charged with a crime it might fairly have been contended that he knew the difference between right and wrong.

As I have said already, a civil act is destroyed by proof that the person performing it was at the time subject to mental delusion upon one subject, although in every other perfectly reasonable. The only principle upon which this rule can be founded is that the mind is one and entire, and if diseased it is impossible, whatever may be the external signs, to say to what extent, and in what direction, the disease extends. If this be good reasoning, surely it is equally applicable to the mind of a person charged with a crime. I cannot think that, where an insane delusion is clearly proved, although numerous facts may be brought forward to show that the lunatic distinguished, up to the time of the offence, the difference between right and wrong, that he ought to be consigned to the gallows. The gout that has taken possession of a man's toe suddenly leaps to his heart. When a man believes himself to be the Saviour, how is it possible for human skill to tell what thought or opinion is likely to control any act of his life? The law must yield to the dispensations of Providence,.

however much prejudice and passion may seek to sway its administration.

I was witness of the result of the outcry that Drummond's assassination occasioned in a case tried before Baron Alderson at the Central Criminal Court. That very learned judge summed up strongly for an acquittal upon the ground of insanity. The jury, however, took the matter into their own hands and convicted the prisoner. The judge made urgent recommendations to the Home Secretary, but, nevertheless, the man was executed. It will not, I think, be uninteresting to record here one or two cases involving these questions, and in which I have at different periods of my career been engaged as counsel. One of them was of a very distressing character.

A lady of the name of Ramsbottom, the wife of an eminent physician, herself of middle age and generally respected, was suspected of pilfering from a draper's shop in Baker Street, Portman Square. She was watched, followed, and her person was searched, and several small articles were found concealed in different parts of her dress. She was given into custody, went through the painful ordeal of an inquiry at the Marylebone Police Court, and was committed for trial at the Middlesex sessions. At the period when this occurred, Mr. Serjeant Adams was the presiding judge. He was thoroughly impartial and knew all the law necessary for his position, but it was not very well packed in the receptacle of his brain, and the particles constantly came out at wrong times and places. The case, however, could hardly have been confused, the facts were perfectly clear, the whole of the lady's life, as far as its history was known, was not only free from reproach, but thoroughly rational. The only point that could be relied upon for the defence was that the articles stolen were so trivial that no sane object could exist for intentional theft, and the only suggestion that could be made in her favour was that she was not responsible for her actions, being compelled by an uncontrollable impulse, or, to use a technical term, that she was the victim of kleptomania, not a very popular defence before a jury of tradesmen. However, after having been locked up for some hours, they were ultimately discharged without giving a verdict, a result arising probably more from compassion for the lady's husband than any doubt about the facts.

I thought at the time that if, instead of laying a trap for her, the proprietor of the shop had conveyed a hint either to herself or to the doctor, it would have been the kinder course, and subsequent circumstances showed that in reality her conduct was attributable to insane influences, although certainly she knew thoroughly well that she was acting wrongly.

She died very shortly after the ordeal she had undergone, broken down in health and spirit with the shame and disgrace, and I was consulted, after her death had taken place, by Dr. Ramsbottom under the following circumstances. Every drawer and cupboard in the house was found to be full of new goods, which she must have been in the habit of abstracting during many years, and I believe that in every instance they were contained in their original wrappers. Mrs. Ramsbottom was a religious woman, and I cannot doubt that every Sunday she listened with respect and veneration to the lessons taught in church, and fully realised the commandment of 'Thou shalt not steal.' And it is clear that she by the acts she committed incurred danger and obtained no advantage. I advised Dr. Ramsbottom not to make the discovery public, and the articles found were distributed amongst different charitable institutions.

Can any one doubt that insanity irresistibly controlled her conduct?

Many instances are upon record in which this extraordinary mania is alleged to have developed itself. And one case is known where an attendant always accompanied a lady of high rank when she went out shopping and paid for the articles she stole. Supposing in any of these instances the parties had committed a crime of a different description, would it be just to hold them responsible? The question is not unimportant, as such acts, if clearly proved, would, as the law now stands, invalidate a will.

Certainly the most remarkable and interesting case connected with mental derangement, in which I acted as counsel, was in connection with the will of a lady named Thwaites. She died at an advanced age, leaving a very large fortune, which she bequeathed to different persons with whom she had associated during her lifetime, and none of whom were her relatives; and her next of kin disputed the will upon the ground that she was insane at the time of making it.

She had inherited the fortune in early life, unexpectedly, upon the death of her husband, and had administered it with judgment and discretion. She was neither niggardly nor profuse. She was charitable without being reckless, and kept her accounts, which were somewhat complicated, with accuracy and in excellent order. No restraint of any kind was ever placed upon her. She played whist, and, I am told, played it fairly well. She endured pain on different occasions with great resignation,[1] and moreover there was nothing extraordi-

[1] Dr. Turner, an old friend of mine and a physician of great

nary in the disposition of her property, as she had never held much intercourse with her own relatives.

Unquestionably, however, she was guilty of some very extraordinary proceedings, and expressed some singular views. She asserted that she had been chosen by our Saviour to receive Him upon His return to earth, and that this event would therefore occur during her lifetime, and she indicated the reality of this belief by making very extensive preparations for His reception, principally in the upholstery line, and there was a great deal of absurdity exhibited in the arrangements she made. Lord Penzance, before whom the case was tried, left it to the jury to say whether she was labouring under an insane delusion, and they found that she was, and he accordingly held that her will was invalid. The circumstances of this case suggest reflections as to how far religious opinions, absurd and ridiculous as they may appear to others, are to be accepted as proof of insanity. The main idea, round which every thought and act rotated in her mind, was the approaching return of the Saviour to earth. This surely cannot be treated as insane. The notion that she was selected to receive Him might be the product of vanity and the misunderstanding of some of the mysterious passages that

eminence at Brighton, gave me an account of her great patience under suffering.

occur in portions of the Scripture, whilst the preparations she made were only the natural consequences of such a belief on the part of a person of utterly unrefined ideas ; and it is to be noted that she was a woman of no education, and from her earliest youth had been the object of fulsome attentions and flattery.[1]

But a grave doubt has occurred to me as to whether the belief in question really had full and undivided possession of her mind, and whether there was not rather a pride in putting forward the claim. She sacrificed nothing of personal interest and comfort, and never appeared to undervalue the good things of this world in consequence of the great honour that was in store for her.

These speculations, however, are beside my main object in discussing the subject. For that purpose I assume that a delusion, utterly inconsistent with sanity, had taken possession of her senses, and that, therefore, she was unfit to execute any legal document. In what manner ought she to have been dealt with if she had committed what in a sane, person would have been a crime? Her whole life showed that she understood the distinction between right and wrong; and if the issue

---

[1] Sir Roundell Palmer led me upon the first trial, and his speech is well worth the perusal of those who desire to look deeply into this subject.

left to a jury had been narrowed to that question, unless the fact that she was under a delusion upon the subject of the Saviour's returning to earth and becoming her guest could be treated as evidence that she was unable to tell right from wrong, she must have been convicted.

I have been engaged in many cases of interest since the constitution of the Probate and Divorce Court before the three judges who have severally presided, and, amongst others, the very unhappy one of Lady Mordaunt. This unfortunate lady became insane after a confinement, and continued hopelessly so from that period. This was an instance where the mind was entirely destroyed, and therefore it presented none of those difficulties which I have pointed out in other cases, and which I venture to think deserve the attention both of those who make the laws and those who administer them.

Having mentioned the Court of Probate and Divorce, this may not be an improper place to allude to its formation and the judges who have presided in it. When first constituted, Mr. Justice Cresswell, then a member of the Court of Common Pleas, was selected as its head, and it would have been difficult to make a better choice. He was a most able lawyer and a man of the world. He had been a successful leader at the bar, was an acute cross-examiner, and an utter despiser of all shams. He narrowly watched the demeanour of the witnesses who gave evidence before him, and usually formed just conclusions. I wish I could finish my sketch without a word of reproach or blame, but, in justice, I must say that his manner was too often supercilious, thus detracting from his high qualities. At the same time he was eminently just, and never carried any feeling he might have shown against either counsel or witness into the comments that he made to the jury, and his perfect impartiality will, I am sure, be admitted and remembered by everyone who knew him. He tried one very remarkable probate case, in which I opposed a will propounded by a person named Smethurst, presenting features which I think are of a very singular character. This man succeeded in upholding the will, which I attribute to one of the most admirable speeches I ever heard from Dr., now Sir Robert, Phillimore, who was his counsel.

Lord Penzance, a Baron of the Exchequer, succeeded Cresswell, who died from the result of an accident. He possessed all the high judicial qualities of his predecessor, whilst his demeanour was most courteous to everyone, and, if it was his duty to differ from counsel, he did so with good taste and gentlemanly bearing. He had mixed much in the world, and thus obtained that knowledge which in the Divorce Court is peculiarly, required. It was a matter of sincere regret when, in consequence of ill health, he was obliged to retire from the office.

It would not become me to discuss the merits of Sir James Hannen, the present presiding judge, but I may say that I have been engaged with and against him in many cases whilst he was at the bar, and I never knew a more conscientious or painstaking advocate.

CHAPTER XXI.

TRIAL OF BARBER AND FLETCHER.

In the month of April 1844 a trial took place at the Central Criminal Court which brought to light a very elaborate and complicated system of fraud. The parties alleged to have been engaged in it were a person of the name of Fletcher, who was by profession a medical man, an attorney of the name of Barber, and three women. The forgery of wills and the personation of individuals was the basis of the different transactions. No doubt whatever exists as to Fletcher having been largely and criminally engaged in them ; but Barber alleged that he had acted simply in a legal capacity without any knowledge of the character of the acts. Fletcher also from the commencement entirely exculpated him, and there was nothing to show that he derived any profit except such as he was entitled to for his professional charges. At the same time it was difficult to account for a shrewd man of business being mixed up in so many transactions as were proved against Barber without his having a suspicion of their nature. The prosecution was conducted by Sir Frederick Pollock on the part of the Bank of England. A very excellent lawyer of the name of Graves (who is recently dead), with myself, defended Fletcher, and for him the only hope could be from some technical point, which, however, all the ingenuity and legal acumen of my leader were unable to discover, and he was unhesitatingly found guilty.

Barber was defended by Wilkins, a gentleman whose qualities I have already described. The judge who tried the case was Mr. Baron Gurney, who had obtained for himself the reputation of being very harsh and severe in his administration of justice, and certainly his manner warranted the opinion. I do not remember that whilst presiding upon this trial he did anything that could invite censure ; but Wilkins made a most bitter attack upon him in the course of his speecn The words he used, as far as I can remember them, were as follows: 'There exist those upon the bench who have the character of convicting judges. I do not envy their reputation in this world or their fate hereafter.' Mr. Baron Gurney was at this time an old man and in feeble health, and Sir John Bailey, who was one of the junior counsel for the prosecution and a great friend of the baron, told me that he felt the attack very much. I do not consider that the position of a barrister could justify expressions of such a character, and, although his client was acquitted on this occasion, I cannot help thinking that when he was subsequently tried on another case this attack was not forgotten. I can, however, very well remember that early in my career it was with fear and trembling that I appeared as counsel before the object of them.

Mr. Baron Gurney, when at the bar, possessed great power and cleverness in dealing with facts, a quality which also distinguished him upon the bench ; but certainly he had earned the reputation of being a very pitiless judge, and his manner at times was almost brutal, and already in these pages I have more than once expressed my opinion of how grave a defect this is in those who have to administer justice.

In early life Mr. Gurney was nearly a rebel, but it will be more polite to describe him as a very advanced Liberal ; as, however, he progressed in the profession the vivifying light of Toryism began to affect his senses, and before he arrived at the bench high Church and State doctrines had taken firm root in his mind. He must often have lamented that when he named his children he had not been endowed with the spirit of prophecy, as certainly in that case they would have sailed under very different names than those of Russell, Hampden, and

Sidney. The first of these gentlemen afterwards filled the office of Recorder of London ; he possessed all his father's clearness and precision, with great gentleness of manner and kindness of heart. He did the greatest credit to the corporation who elected him, and it will be long before his loss is forgotten.

After the acquittal of Barber, both prisoners were again put upon their trial for uttering the forged will of a lady named Ann Slack. In the interval, however, between the two trials a change had taken place. Mr. Justice John Williams presided, and Sir Frederick Pollock having become Lord Chief Baron, Mr. Erle, afterwards Chief Justice of the Common Pleas, conducted the prosecution. This gentleman did not possess eloquence, and suffered from a slight impediment in his speech, but was nevertheless a very acute and able advocate. As I was still representing Fletcher, although his fate was sealed, I watched the conduct of the case very carefully. Mr. Erle laboured the strong parts against Barber, and contrived almost to make it appear that he was the *fons et origo* of the whole conspiracy. Wilkins made a very indifferent defence, and Mr. Justice Williams simply followed in the most servile manner the lead of the counsel for the prosecution. Both prisoners were convicted, and sentenced to transportation for life. As regards Barber, the verdict was most unjust, for

without affirming his absolute innocence, it is
impossible to say that there was not very grave
doubt as to his guilt.   After Barber had been sent
out of the country in pursuance of his sentence and
had undergone great hardships, he was pardoned,
and received some compensation.   I often saw him
during the short period that he survived his return,
his tall form gaunt and haggard, and the sufferings
he had undergone stamped upon his features.   He
must have been an object of pity to everyone
possessed of human sympathy.

Johnny Williams, so everyone called him,
except when he was ' my lord,' had been one of
the counsel for Queen Caroline, associated with
Brougham and Denman.   His knowledge of the
Italian language was supposed to have been the
reason why he was selected for that position, as he
had not held any distinguished place at the bar.
I fancy his business was pretty much confined to
criminal cases, in the conduct of which he had
the reputation of sharpness and sagacity.   He was
much given to strong expletives, which in the
following anecdotes I must be excused for omitting.

Upon the trial of a prisoner for a capital
charge, he had been induced by the urgency of an
attorney, although against his own opinion, to ask a
question, the answer to which convicted his client.
Turning to the attorney, he said, emphasising as may

be imagined every word with strong additions: 'Go
home, cut your throat, and *when* you meet your
client in H—— beg his pardon.' Another story
told of him is that a clerk, recently married, hanged
himself. Another person who afterwards entered
his employment expressed a hope that Johnny
would not be offended at his entering into the
holy bonds of matrimony. 'Certainly not,' said
he. 'Marry by all means; but *when* you hang
yourself do not do so in my chambers,' which
his former clerk had done. He was a capital
shot, and whilst enjoying the sport upon some
gentleman's preserves, and knocking over the
birds right and left, the gamekeeper whispered
confidentially to his comrade, 'They tell me this
'ere gent is a judge. I'll take my Bible oath he has
been a poacher.'

Mr. Erle became, as is well known, puisné judge
in the Court of Queen's Bench, and afterwards Lord
Chief Justice of the Court of Common Pleas. He
possessed a very judicial manner, thorough independence, and an earnest desire to secure justice in the
cases he tried. He was, however, very obstinate,
and when once he had formed an opinion it was
almost impossible to get him to change it. His
experience in life had given him but little knowledge of some of its by-paths. He put too much
faith in outside respectability, and was almost as

weak as some juries in cases where injuries were alleged to have been inflicted upon women. Upon one occasion at Guildford, when I was engaged to defend a prisoner upon a charge of this description, I ventured respectfully but strongly and earnestly to allude to this, which I considered an infirmity of his mind, and I referred to cases in which I thought injustice had been done. In summing up he commented with a good deal of emotion upon my observations, but gave me credit for sincerity. In a former chapter I have alluded to this case, which resulted in an acquittal owing to the impressive caution which, I venture to think, I caused him to introduce into his charge to the jury.

I was counsel in the last cause that he tried, and his dealing with it illustrated what I have said about his want of knowledge of the ways of the world. It was an action arising out of the sale of a horse, for which my client had given three hundred guineas. It was a magnificent-looking animal, and had been shown off by a very pretty girl before it was purchased. The horse was a screw, and the whole affair a plant. The Chief Justice was indignant at my defence. He could see nothing to justify the imputations I had made, and so he summed up. The jury, however, with very little hesitation, found in favour of my client. I met Erle leaving the court. He was greatly

vexed at the verdict, and could not understand it.
I told him that the parties probably were known
to the jury, but I cannot help thinking that he
felt his power and influence were waning. His predecessor, Sir John Jervis, would have seen through
the whole fraud in a moment.

Whatever may have been his deficiencies, and
although the Court of Common Pleas has been
presided over by most distinguished judges, none
ever sat upon the bench who left behind him a
higher character for the most unswerving integrity.

He was a man of great benevolence, and I have
heard many anecdotes indicative of his kindness of
heart, and one example happened to come within
my own knowledge. He was presiding in the Civil
Court at Northampton, and was obliged to direct
a jury against some poor people who had been
scandalously but legally swindled. To them the
result was absolute ruin. On the following morning an elderly gentleman on horseback made his
appearance in the alley where the sufferers resided.
This was Sir William Erle. He gave them some
very good advice, and with it a sum of money that
replaced them in their old position.

Having, as I have already mentioned, a slight
impediment in his speech, he had contracted a habit
of looking into the air instead of into the faces

of his audience. The effect of this was peculiar. After his retirement from the bench he went to live in the country, where he enjoyed himself for many years, and died at an advanced age. The last time that I saw him was when I was counsel in the Petersfield Election Committee; the place was near his residence, and he came over and took his seat beside Mr. Justice Mellor, who was the judge. I need not say that he was cordially recognised by such members of the bar as were present. I took the opportunity of quoting one of his decisions in the Court of Common Pleas which was, I fancy, bad law. Very quietly he got hold of the report from which I had quoted. Of course he could not interfere, but I fancied that his look was almost agonised when Mr. Justice Mellor decided the point mainly I believe out of compliment to him.

Sir William Erle had been a member of the Western Circuit, and it is no unpleasing task to record the eminent men whose early professional life commenced upon it: Sir William Follett, Mr. Justice Crowder, Lord Chief Justice Cockburn, Sir Montague Smith, Sir Robert Collier, and now Lord Chief Justice Coleridge. But not less in ability, and in all those qualities which make a man loved and respected, was a gentleman whose premature death has deprived the profession of one of its greatest ornaments.

When first I met Sir John Karslake he was one of the gayest and brightest of a pleasant circle at the house of Mrs. Crealock, in Stanhope Place, Hyde Park. He speedily attained a very high position at the bar, and no rank was so exalted that he might not have fairly aspired to it. He broke down from over-conscientiousness. He was never satisfied that he had done enough for a client, and he wore himself out by labour and anxiety where an equally successful result might have been attained at a much less cost.

I have been with him in cases from which his attention never flagged, although his brain was being racked by the most horrible of agonies. No wonder he succumbed.

The last time that I was with him was in an action brought by, I think, the Italian Government against an English firm for breach of contract in the supply of boots for the army. He was suffering fearfully, and I was very anxious to relieve him of the work, which it was quite within my power to do, but I could not prevail upon him to accept the slightest help. It must have been some, though a sad, satisfaction to his oldest friend to offer the tribute to his memory which appeared lately in a morning journal, and which those who read it will admit was by no means overcharged. [1]

[1] A letter from Lord Coleridge, referring to Sir John Karslake, appeared in the *Times* newspaper of the date of October 10, 1881.

CHAPTER XXII.

CAMPDEN HOUSE FIRE.

In 1862 Campden House was a feature at Kensington. It was occupied by a Mr. and Mrs. Woolley, who received a good deal of company, and were said to be persons of wealth. The parties they gave would now be called æsthetic.

Mr. Woolley was himself a confirmed invalid, his eyesight defective, and he could scarcely move about without the assistance of a valet. In the commencement of the above year, and in the middle of the night, a fire broke out upon the premises. It spread with singular rapidity, and consumed the whole of them with their alleged valuable contents. The property was insured in different offices to the aggregate amount of 30,000*l.*, and the companies disputed the payment. They alleged that Mr. Woolley was in distressed circumstances, that the amount of property in the house was grossly exaggerated, and that he had himself set fire to it in pursuance of an elaborate system of fraud. They alleged that his apparent

feebleness was simulated for the purpose of successfully carrying it out. It was clear, if he
really was the invalid he appeared to be, that
their theory must be abandoned; and if he were
shamming, that he must have contrived to keep up
the appearance for a considerable time before executing his contemplated design.

He brought an action against the Sun Insurance
Company, it being arranged that all the other
claims should stand or fall by the result. It came
on to be tried at the Croydon summer assizes, before
Mr. Baron Bramwell. Mr. Bovill, myself, Mr. James
(the present Attorney-General), and a Mr. Rosher
were counsel for Mr. Woolley. Mr. Lush, the
late Lord Justice (I forget who was with him),
represented the company.

There were many circumstances that justified
the resistance of the claims, and it was pretty clear
that the result would turn upon the mode in which
Mr. Woolley underwent examination. If he was
playing a part, he was the very best actor that I
ever saw. He was unshaken by the cross-examination, and his painful infirmities secured the sympathy of the jury, who found a verdict in his
favour, which was not subsequently disturbed.

A rather amusing incident occurred in connection with the case. The fire had broken out
after midnight, and a gentleman saw and reported

it ; but when the question arose of calling him as
a witness, he protested against our doing so, as it
would inform some inquisitive connections where
he was on that morning, which, for some reason, he
had a very strong objection to. It occurred to me
that his evidence might be admitted, and I sounded
Lush upon the subject, and learnt that there was a
witness in his brief who had exactly a similar
objection, and so we agreed that the two should
pair off together, and we called neither of them ;
and I believe that this benevolent arrangement
prevented some little inconvenience in two domestic
circles.

The assizes for the Home Circuit were held
every alternate year at Croydon, and for many
years I was accustomed to lodge with two worthy
old people, who kept a small shoemaker's shop in
the High Street ; very honest they were, and kindly,
and professedly Christians of great strictness, but
of the not uncommon denomination of those from
whose creed charity is expunged. I was engaged
for the prosecution at an assizes many years ago of
a young German charged with murder ; and for
the purpose of tracing the alleged murderer it was
necessary to call the celebrated singer, Madame
Titiens, who had afforded him pecuniary relief after
the commission of the act. I had known this lady
for some years, and always entertained the greatest

respect for her character as well as admiration for her talents and accomplishments. She was extremely generous, and her own country-people especially were always sure of assistance. It was this reputation that had induced the accused to apply to her. As is well known, the hotels during the assizes are very full, and I invited Madame Titiens and her niece to occupy my lodgings whilst she was waiting to be called. On the following day my old landlady gave me notice to quit, saying ' she would have no stage players in her house.' Madame Titiens had a pretty little residence in the Finchley Road, where I have often enjoyed most pleasant evenings. Amongst those whom I was in the habit of meeting was Signor Giuglini, the wonderful tenor. His career was but a short one : the climate of Russia and a habit he unfortunately contracted of taking stimulants destroyed his nervous system, and for some time he was an inmate of the asylum kept by my old friend Dr. Tuke at Turnham Green But there was no hope of recovery. Madame Titiens frequently called upon him there and took him out for a drive. He was perfectly harmless, and not discontented with his lot, expressing himself grateful for the kindness he received from the doctor. He ultimately was sent into Italy, where he died. Many also were the pleasant parties in which I met Madame Titiens at the Star and Garter at Richmond, not then the great ugly staring barrack of a place that occupies the site where Mr. Ellis, the picture of a host, used to receive the guests. The old house was burnt down. In itself it had not much pretension, but the garden behind was a perfect picture of loveliness; the small garden-rooms, with honeysuckles, jasmine, and roses twining themselves up the sides, with a lovely sweep of lawn, on which were scattered trees that had flourished there for many a long day, affording shade as well as beauty; one magnificent spreading beech, itself a sight, and an avenue of limes forming the prettiest of walks at the bottom of the garden, with a view beyond : none fairer to be seen through the length and breadth of England. A company possessed themselves of it. To their eyes and imaginations nothing was so beautiful as bricks and mortar. The trees were in the way, and have been cleared off; in the place of flowers that seemed to flourish of their own free will, formal beds are stiffly planted. The dear old lime-walk is supplanted by a terrace without an atom of shade, and which is not improved by the perfume of the stables, over which it has been constructed. No modern improver can ever make Richmond otherwise than beautiful, but the loveliness of the Star and Garter is one of the things of the past. The very obliging manager of the hotel is not responsible for the vandalisms that have changed the fair scene that existed into its present shape, and as far as attention and good fare will satisfy the visitor he will have no reason to complain. On a Sunday the garden was usually crowded. Artists and singers, whose avocations kept them in London during the week, revelled in the landscape, and amongst them I have often enjoyed it; and there were representatives of every other class, well-known figures of the literary, political, and social worlds. There was a party I well remember in connection with one of the most delightful days of many that I passed there; it consisted of Balfe the composer, and his surpassingly lovely daughter, whose career was so short. She was twice married; once to Sir J. Crampton, who I think was our ambassador to the Court of Russia, and afterwards to a grandee of Spain, and died when quite young. Mowbray Morris was another of the group. He was manager of the 'Times' newspaper, and with him I was very intimate. I was his counsel in a case that caused him anxiety and pain, but ended successfully for him. The fourth of the group in addition to myself was Mr. Delane, the editor of the same paper, and upon the shoulders of these two men rested the entire weight of its management. No one could be in the society of the latter gentleman without feeling that he was a man of the age.

There was a quiet power in his conversation, his knowledge was very varied, and a vein of agreeable *persiflage* adorned and lightened whatever he talked about. The last time I met him was at a dinner party at Dr. Quain's, the eminent physician.

At that time his mind had partially given way under the attacks of incurable disease, and it was painful to witness how occasional were the flashes of an intellect that in former days was wont to shed so bright and lasting a light. On this occasion his brougham came for him at the time it had been his custom to go to the office, and he still had the idea that he was actively engaged, although the real editorship had passed into other hands. It seems so short a time since we five were stretched upon the grass plot in full health and spirits, and now I alone of all that party am left to recall it.

Another of whom I am obliged to speak in the past, and with whom I have passed at the Star and Garter, as well as elsewhere, many a pleasant hour, was Charles Lever, the author of 'Harry Lorrequer' and other works of fiction; a bright, well-educated, witty Irishman. His stories at table were as amusing and improbable as many that came from his pen. I believe he was a member of the Garrick Club, but I do not remember ever meeting him there. I cannot recall whether it has been at

some of the pleasant gatherings in those old days
that I have met George Augustus Sala. Wherever
it was, I know that he added fully his share to the
joyousness of the party. Every one has read his
graphic sketches of different phases of London life,
and amusing details of travels abroad ; but not so
many his very clever novel of the ' Seven Sons of
Mammon,' which I think bears comparison with
most of the fictions of the day.[1] Amongst others
from whose society this pleasant resort derived an
additional charm were Signor and Madame Arditi,
with whom I was fortunate enough to form an
acquaintance shortly after their arrival in this
country, and I believe it was upon my invitation
that they, for the first time, made its acquaintance,
and, since that period, in their company I have
often and much enjoyed myself. I have been glad,
in concluding the brief sketch that I have ventured
upon of this hotel, and after bemoaning the destruction of honeysuckles and rose-trees and the
barbarous disfigurement of a favourite spot, and
mourning over departed friends, to be able to refer
to those who are still living, and affording pleasure
to a large circle of friends, and to express a hope
that they may long continue to do so.

[1] In it will be found the apprehension of his heroine, by a French
detective, on the Derby race-course, which equals, in skill and
power, any sensational incident that I have ever read.

CHAPTER XXIII.

EVANS'S.

LET me now change the scene and present my readers to one of a very different description, although there are many to be found here who might have been seen on the preceding Sunday enjoying the pleasures of the Star and Garter.

It is the interior of a large hall, and the hour about midnight. The atmosphere is thickened by smoke. There are numerous tables, at which gentlemen are seated taking refreshments. The walls are covered with paintings of celebrated actors and actresses, and upon a raised platform at the further end of the room are some dozen boys singing with taste and accuracy a popular glee. Moving amongst the tables, upon legs rather shaky, a rotund figure with a rubicund face and yellow wig offers with much courtesy his snuffbox to the occupiers, hoping at the same time that they have been supplied with all they want. The hall is Evans's, Covent Garden. Since I last saw it, twenty years ago, it is much changed; a handsome edifice is added to the long

room of which it consisted when Colonel Newcome
left it in disgust at the obscenity that went on.
The owner of the snuff-box is the proprietor of the
hall, and to him is due the change in its character
that has taken place. It is now conducted with
perfect propriety, the amusements are refined, and
the refreshments good and moderate. My readers
will recognise Mr. Green, Paddy, as he was always
called behind his back, and by those who knew
him well in speaking to him. Originally he had
appeared upon the stage at the Adelphi, not, I
fancy, in a higher capacity than a chorus-singer;
and in the days that I have previously spoken of
he sang at the old rooms, not, however, any songs
that were reprehensible; although I must, I am
afraid, admit that he was present during the time
that they were sung, and when reminded of the improprieties of those days he would shake his head
gravely; but as he was a devout Catholic, I have no
doubt he had obtained absolution. I used to take a
great deal of pleasure in his conversation. He was
possessed of a very retentive memory, and could relate, and did so pleasantly, many scenes of London
life. Artists, lawyers, writers, actors, and men of
fashion congregated in the hall of a night, and in a
corner of what once was formerly the old room a
circle of friends used to meet, and in cheerful and
not unintellectual gossip spend much agreeable time.

Paddy was very proud, and might not unreasonably be so, of some who joined this group.

There was also a gallery, the visitors to which were concealed by trellis-work, and to this ladies were admitted, and here they could listen to the songs and eat suppers supposed generally to be confined to the other sex. Paddy also prided himself upon these visits, and recorded with much gusto the names of distinguished guests; and it was a well-known fact in the establishment that royalty had condescended to accept a pinch of snuff from his hospitable box.

Another personage, scarcely of less interest than Mr. Green himself, was always to be seen in the rooms. He also wandered from table to table, and was received with a welcome by the *habitués*. He professed to sell cigars, but when the eye of his chief was not upon him he would pull out of his pocket a well-worn card, and express a hope that the visitor would honour his concert which was shortly about to come off; but no one ever lived who witnessed it. This was Herr von Joel, once upon a time a popular singer in refined circles.

He used to sing Swiss mountain melodies. He also whistled and imitated birds very naturally, and towards the end of an evening would give an amusing imitation of a farmyard. He sang one night;

the next he did not appear, nor the next, and on the following we heard that he was dead.

Mr. Green retired from its management, and it gradually sank in character. Now the building has become the property of a club to which has been given the name of the Falstaff, it is to be hoped that some of the old associations may be revived, and from what I know of the subscribers I think that the wish may be fulfilled.

I was a favourite with Mr. Green, and one chair was always kept for me. I belonged to several clubs, but during the years I am now dwelling upon there were no meetings so convivial as these, and the faces to be seen in the room, even if the visitor was not in direct communion with them, were pleasant to behold. Thackeray was constantly there: he was not social, but people liked to be in apparent company with the great novelist. He sat apart generally, wrapt in contemplation. Charles Dickens would flit in only rarely, but always in apparently good spirits, and glad to respond to the many words of welcome he received. Albert Smith, after he had descended from Mont Blanc at the Egyptian Hall, never missed the pleasant reunion, and there were none who came amongst us more deservedly popular than he and his brother. I have met Douglas Jerrold there. To him I have before alluded. I have seen him in company with men of great ability, but I never saw anyone who, for a short period, sparkled so much ; but, meteor-like, he too soon sank into darkness. Shirley Brooks was often amongst us. I need say no more of him than I have already done. A very constant guest was Robertson, the creator of a style of drama which, with the assistance of Mrs. Bancroft's talent, has filled with splendid audiences a theatre which for years before had wooed in vain the patronage of the public. Poor Robertson died only too early, almost before he could witness the triumphs of his sister Mrs. Kendal, one of the most fascinating actresses of the present day.

Quaint little Buckstone would sometimes hop in, and excite amusement and fun apparently without intention. I think it was here that I was introduced to Mr. Barry, an Irish barrister, since Attorney-General, and now judge, and from whom I have since received a substantial mark of friendship. There was one amongst those I met who fills a melancholy space upon the page of history; I allude to Prince Maximilian. Paddy Green took me up to him one night whilst he was indulging in a tankard of ale, and introduced me to him very effusively, and we met on other evenings and drank beer together. He was very unaffected, although with a reserved manner. I cannot help thinking, though possibly this may result from after events, that there was upon the countenance of the future Emperor of Mexico a cloud that seemed to foretell his melancholy fate.

And there was another, not so illustrious and not known to history, whose fate was fully as sad. This was Mr. Boultby, a man of great ability, engaged upon the staff of the 'Times' newspaper. He had suffered many troubles, about which he had consulted me, and I entertained for him a sincere friendship. One night very late we were seated together at Evans's; on the following day he was to start for China, to which place he had accepted the post of correspondent with the English army.

He was not in high spirits, and told me that it was only for the sake of those dependent upon him that he went. He sailed, as he had proposed, on the following day, and joined the army. Shortly after his arrival there was an engagement in which our troops had been victorious. My friend, with some companions, rode on in advance of the main body, and being surprised were all of them taken prisoners by the Chinese. They were subjected to frightful tortures, from which poor Boultby died, In the far distant land a monument has been erected to his memory, and the object for which he sacrificed his life has been attained through the liberality of those he served.

It is only very recently that a well-known face is missing from the tables of those who love the society of artists, and old as he was when he passed away from the scenes of his successes, his death caused surprise, for he had looked for so many years the same, his cheery spirits never seemed to flag, and he appeared to have defied the inevitable.

This was Planché. I knew him well and met him often. I suppose that in his long journey through life, although he met with great success, he never made an enemy; and though many of his contemporaries might be named whose literary fame is greater, how few have caused more amusement! He was, moreover, fortunate in being associated with Madame Vestris, who seemed to be created to embody upon the stage, and even to give additional charm to his refined and elegant burlesques.

There was another friend of mine who defied age, whose good temper and high spirits never flagged, who could have been an eminent architect, who was an accomplished painter, but who preferred the stage and its trials; this was Charles Mathews.

The fame of his father, and the popularity that from his earliest age he had himself obtained, secured him a reception on the first night of his appearance at the Olympic Theatre never before equalled by any actor. The promise he then gave he entirely fulfilled, and within six months of his death he drew large houses and played with vigour and spirit. I had a very agreeable meeting with him and his accomplished wife upon one of my visits to Homburg, and I remember with pleasure a dinner that I gave to them at the Hôtel de Russie, at Frankfort, and afterwards how the actor, who himself never failed when he desired it to excite fun and merriment, laughed most heartily at the tricks of a clown in a circus to which we all adjourned after an excellent repast.

I have in a former chapter mentioned meeting Macready, but I had no particular acquaintance with him. He was a conscientious manager, a scholar and a gentleman, but fractious and overbearing. Such, at least, was his reputation. I cannot say I think he was a good delineator of Shakespeare's characters. The one which, in my opinion, he played best was Prospero, in the 'Tempest.' I was present one night, the first that it was played at Covent Garden Theatre, when a young lady made her appearance in Ariel. She was wafted across the stage, and sang, with exquisite sweetness, the well-known song commencing 'Where the bee sucks.' This was received with rounds of applause, and practically raised her into the prominent feature of the play. This was Miss Priscilla Horton, then

scarcely known, but who has since been continu-
ously gathering laurels as Mrs. German Reed. I
could not hope to recall to the memory of those
who have witnessed the extravaganzas of Planché
their effect upon the audience, or to give an idea
of it to others who have not, without naming a
performer who was of no small assistance to them.
The most blustering he was of monarchs : his swagger conveyed a volume, and so did his voice, which
he used with infinite effect and humour. This was
a gentleman named Bland, and he, like Madame
Vestris, seemed to have been created for the special
illustration of Planché's genius.

In the allusions I have made to members of
a profession from all of whom I have met with
much kindness, and amongst whom I have enjoyed so many pleasant hours, I need hardly say
I have been governed solely by the memories that
have presented themselves to my mind, and not
with any notion of exhausting the subject ; and I
have not ventured to refer to those with whom I
still have the pleasure of an acquaintance, lest the
sincere terms I should be obliged to use might
cause me to be accused of flattery.

There are public performers who do not strictly
belong to the theatrical profession, and with one of
these I happened in a business matter to be brought
into contact. He was an acrobat, and plaintiff in an

action for breach of contract. I was much struck
with the amount of simple truthfulness that he
displayed in giving evidence, and asked him to call
upon me, which he did. I was curious to learn
something of a life of so exceptional a character.
He was a sinewy little fellow, and born into the
world in the name of Martin, but he called himself
Martini. His brother, he told me, was just dead,
and he was looking out for another, not a real
brother, but a professional one. His last brother
was named Jones, and he had fallen from the
trapeze and broken his neck. ' You see,' he said
in relating the story, 'it is very difficult to get
suited, as we may not know each other's tricks.'
He was quite aware, he said, of the dangers of his
profession, but then the salary was large and he
hoped to save enough in two or three years to
retire. He ate no meat whilst under an engagement, and never took stimulants at any time.
He told me of some shocking accidents, where
the sufferers were only crippled, and said that they
were usually occasioned by the carelessness of the
people employed in the performances. Exhibitions
of the sort that this poor fellow described are a
scandal to a civilised country.[1] My friend, however, was by no means despondent, and considered
his branch of the profession much higher than that

---

[1] *Vide* Appendix.

of gymnasts who did not risk their lives. Whatever we may think of the taste that encourages the latter class of performers, their exhibition does not, at all events, shock humanity. My client won his verdict, but whether he succeeded in finding another relative, or what became of him afterwards, I never heard. I once remember, during a pantomime at Drury Lane, a great professor of what he called gymnastic art. He wore a mask of truly satanic appearance, and three urchins, representing imps, assisted him in his performance. I saw him between the acts in the green-room. His theatrical head was lying on a table. His own real one was very gentle and mild. The boys were tumbling ; one of them performed an unusually good somersault. 'God will reward you, my boy,' he said, patting him upon his head. Turning to me, he added, 'They are good children. Their mother hears them their prayers night and morning.' It was evident that there was real affection between those four, and that they felt no small pride in their monkey tricks.

I was inducted behind the scenes very early in my life, and have been told that I ran away from Miss Foote, the beautiful actress, when she wanted to kiss me. I have, however, never fully believed this story. I have since known much of the life behind the curtain and of the

heart-aching that is concealed within the glare
and tinsel exposed to the audience, and I believe
that a very wrong estimate is formed of those who
make part of the splendid pageant. The chorus-
singers and ballet-girls are consigned, by the
opinion of those who know little about them, to
much undeserved obloquy. Of course, amongst
them, as in all classes, there are those who merit
this opinion, but I believe the majority are honest,
hard-working girls, and that there is many a
household saved from starvation by their patient
industry.

Those who have known Drury Lane Theatre
as I have done for many years, before and behind
the curtain, will have had great pleasure in the
acquaintance of Mr. Sterling, for long the stage
manager. He was not only most excellent in this
department, but was a thoroughly kind-hearted
though strict disciplinarian. He has confirmed the
opinion that I have expressed of the character of the
employées. Mr. Sterling has recently published an
amusing account of the actors and actresses that
he has known, and is the author of several pleasant
farces. I met him at dinner shortly ago at my
old friend's, Sir Mordaunt Wells, and had a charming gossip about former days. He told me a little
story that pleased me. It was of three young
children who were fairies or angels in the panto-

mime last Christmas. It was on one of the bitter snowy nights, and all the vehicles were off the road. The eldest of the three was only eight years old. The two infants, each clinging to the arm of the elder child, set off to walk to Camberwell, and got there safely. How soon necessity teaches courage and self-reliance! Those who have read the Life of Grimaldi, by Charles Dickens, will have learnt with what agony of body on the part of the performer roars of laughter from the audience are sometimes elicited. The career of these poor fellows is seldom long. Their great muscular exertions, and the draughts they are exposed to, soon bring on disease. The clown of one pantomime may not be seen in the next, but the motley is there, and no one asks for him who wore it last. There have, however, been some who have played for many consecutive years, and I remember a pantaloon with whom I often had a gossip, named Barnes. He was a very sober, decent fellow. Once when I was behind the scenes at Old Drury he told me, almost with tears in his eyes, that he was not to be engaged for the next Christmas. 'And to think,' said he, 'that they have turned me off, although I have played for thirty years, and engaged a mere boy.'

Before I close my theatrical recollections, I must relate an incident in which I placed a most

distinguished and highly respectable friend of mine
in a very embarrassing position. He was induced,
by a desire to add to his knowledge and by my
persuasion, to accompany me behind the scenes
during the performance of a pantomine. To him
the sight was a novel one, and, doubtlessly engaged
in admiration of some of the mechanical effects, he
was unconscious of the flight of time, which I also
disregarded. Suddenly the scene was changed,
and we found ourselves in a storm of carrots,
cabbages, and turnips, which terminated the act,
technically termed, I believe, a ' general rally.'

I will not mention my friend's name, as in the
minds of some highly conscientious people the
contact with a stage cabbage would cause pollution.
Notwithstanding this experience, once again my
friend trusted himself to my care, to drive him
home from a Greenwich dinner. The whitebait,
somehow, had got into my head, and, like myself,
my horses were somewhat fresh. We went at a
spanking pace until suddenly brought to a stand-
still by the pole of my phaeton running through
the back of a costermonger's cart. My friend
declared that I instantly fell fast asleep, and
left him to pacify a furious lady, whose back
had been placed in no small jeopardy. He succeeded in doing so, and I never asked how. He
always had a way with the ladies. We reached home

safely. There was an omnibus that got into our way near St. Martin's Church, but this peril we also escaped, or the country might have lost a valuable servant.

Ought I to forget the first theatrical perform-ancé that I ever beheld, that tyrannical and brutal husband Punch! I did delight, and half believed in him. Now, when I notice the poor fellows whom I see wearily treading the street with the show upon their shoulders, I think of two pic-tures painted by a French artist, entitled 'Avant et Devant,' one representing the laughing audience in front, the other a starving wife and children behind.

CHAPTER XXIV.

ILLUSTRIOUS VISITORS.

In the month of June, in the year of our Lord 1847—I like to make the most of a date when I possess one—I received a visit at my chambers of a very unexpected character. It was from two personages who were then amongst the most noted in London society. One of them was Prince Louis Napoleon; the other the prince of dandies, Count D'Orsay. Of course I knew the former by sight, and with the latter I had some personal acquaintance from having met him at the house of a well known physician, Dr. James Johnson, residing in Suffolk Place, Pall Mall, and with whose family I was upon terms of intimacy.

The object of their visit was to consult me with relation to a fraud of which Prince Louis Napoleon had been made the subject. It appeared that a bill-discounter had, under the pretence of raising money for the Prince, obtained from him two bills of exchange, amounting to 2,000*l*., the proceeds of which he had converted to his own use.

The circumstances were explained to me, and, although there could be no doubt that the Prince had been swindled, the mode in which it had been effected did not bring the perpetrator within the operation of the criminal law; and this to the best of my ability I explained, but I could not convince the Prince, who seemed quite unable to grasp the idea that the law of this country was not regulated by the Code Napoléon. They remained with me for some time, but my arguments had no effect. He reiterated his views with scarcely a change of expression, and seemingly could not get mine into his mind. Shortly after they had left, the Count returned, and expressed himself thoroughly satis- fied with the correctness and wisdom of the advice that I had given, but said that it was useless to argue with the Prince; that he was possessed with one idea upon the subject, and that nothing would remove it. He said that he himself was greatly annoyed, and with some embarrassment offered me a fee; but I declined to treat our conversation in a professional point of view. We parted upon very agreeable terms, and I met him occasionally afterwards.

It would be very presumptuous to assume that upon so short an opportunity I should be capable of forming a correct opinion of the Prince's intel- lect, but there can be no impropriety in expressing

the view left upon my mind at the time ; and this
certainly was not favourable. It seemed to me
that he shrouded himself with a solemn air as if
he was thinking profoundly, but that really it
arose from a slowness of comprehension. Whether
or not the wild exploits of Boulogne and Strasburg
and some other events of his subsequent career
may justify this opinion, I leave it for historians to
determine. He proceeded with the case, and the bill-
discounter was committed for trial at the Central
Criminal Court, which came on before Mr. Baron
Alderson, a learned and very strong judge, and he
at the conclusion of the counsel's opening address
interposed and pointed out the difficulty which I
had in my interview with the Prince attempted to
explain. His counsel was obliged to yield to it, an
acquittal took place, and a scandal was avoided.

I have described Count D'Orsay as the prince
of dandies ; and so he was. I never saw a man
who in personal qualities surpassed him, and his
dress deserved the epithet of artistic. Whether he
was riding through the park, mounted upon a
horse that seemed made to show off his handsome
figure, and which he managed with a grace that
did not in those days distinguish his countrymen,
or he was in the omnibus box at the opera, arrayed,
I must admit, somewhat gorgeously, he always
commanded admiration.

The term dandy conveys to my mind, when associated with those of whom I have read—the Brummells and other characters of the Regency—by no means a pleasant impression. I should have expected to see something grotesquely dressed, with cynical manners and offensive demeanour.

Count D'Orsay was courteous to every one, and kindly. He put the companions of his own sex perfectly at their ease, and delighted them with his varied conversation, and I never saw any one whose manner to ladies was more pleasing and deferential; and I am not ashamed to record the fact that when, as occurred occasionally, he stopped and spoke to me in the park or elsewhere, I used to hope that some of my ordinary companions might witness me in converse with this 'glorious creature.'

It was many years after the circumstances that I have detailed that I again saw Prince Louis Napoleon, and he had then by a wonderful concurrence of events attained the object of his ambition and prophecy. He was Emperor of the French. It was upon the racecourse in the Bois de Boulogne that I then saw him when I was with a party of friends. He noticed me, and sent the Count de Morny to desire that I should be presented to him. He received me with great civility

—I fancy his manner seldom reached cordiality— made no particular allusion to the circumstances of our former meeting, but desired that my friends and myself should be accommodated in what I suppose was the royal stand. He was looking very ill and worn. I never saw him afterwards.

Mr. Baron Alderson was a man worthy of more notice than I have been able to give him from any personal experience. He is one of those designated by Lord Campbell as respectable, and that he deserved that character there is no doubt; but he was in addition a splendid scholar and highly cultivated lawyer. His manner was somewhat brusque, but he was a very humane judge, and, forming an opinion from what I saw of him, almost nervous when trying capital cases. I was counsel in two murder charges before him, in both of which he leant strongly to the side of the accused. One of them was that of a young man, who was acquitted, though certainly guilty, and was afterwards practically proved to be so, being convicted of the robbery which the murderer only could have effected. Alderson's father had been a physician of great eminence at Norwich, one, indeed, of the lights of the profession. I was well acquainted with a son of the Baron's, a very agreeable, gentlemanly person; but the combined talent of the two generations has centred in a female branch.

The counsel who was selected to conduct the prosecution on the part of Prince Napoleon in my place was a gentleman named Humphreys. He was a Queen's Counsel, and leader upon the Midland Circuit. I knew but little of his forensic powers, but I was a witness to the gallant bearing he exhibited under a fearful trial, and happened to be associated with him almost up to the hour of his death. Some eighteen months previously he had been operated upon for cancer. He continued to practise, and upon the occasion I am now referring to I was his junior in a cause before Sir John Jervis in the Court of Common Pleas. Humphreys was suffering intensely, and obliged to conduct it sitting. I learnt, whether from him or not I do not remember, that his daughter was to be married on the following morning. He knew that his end was approaching, and his anxious hope was to live over this marriage.

He left court at four o'clock, and shortly afterwards was found clinging to the rails of Westminster Abbey, was conveyed home, and died during the night. I am able to mention that the marriage which he so much desired to witness took place when the year of mourning had terminated. During the progress of the trial he told the Chief Justice that he had no hope, and that he was so sorry for his clerk. Jervis told him not to trouble himself, and that he would provide for him, which he did after Humphreys' death by giving him an office in the Court of Common Pleas.

The operation to which I have referred was performed by the eminent surgeon whose name has already occurred in these pages, Mr. Lawrence, who sent a report (of course without names) to the ' Lancet.' His patient, who used to read everything upon a subject he was so painfully interested in, recognised that it referred to himself. The concluding words of the report were to this effect : ' The operation was most successful, and will, I trust, prolong life for twelve months.' Another actor in this painful episode soon followed his friend. Sir John Jervis, a man of indomitable pluck, had but a feeble constitution, and it was very painful to witness his sufferings. He was a member, as well as Maule, whom I have already mentioned, of the Union Club, and I have seen him there almost in a state of suffocation from asthma. The incident that I have related of him was by no means the only one that exhibited his kindness of heart.

I was counsel before Mr. Baron Alderson in the case of Sir John Dean Paul, the banker in the

Strand. He was indicted with his partners, Messrs. Strachan and Bates, for embezzling property entrusted to them by their customers. Sir John was believed in by a large circle of confiding friends as the most devout of men, and the evidence upon the trial proved that he certainly was amongst the most fraudulent. They were all three found guilty.

My old friend Henry Allworth Merewether, who had an account with them, is credited with a good joke in connection with their failure. After it had occurred he was coming down the steps of the banking house and nearly tumbled. A friend who happened to be passing expressed a hope that he was not hurt. 'Oh no,' said he, 'I have only lost my balance.'

About the period during which I received the visit that I described at the beginning of this chapter, there might be seen on most afternoons, driving up and down in Hyde Park, an elegantly appointed barouche, and in it two ladies, both strikingly handsome; the one approaching middle age, the other was quite young. These were Lady Blessington and her niece, Miss Power. I knew neither of them, and only introduce their names as their house was the nucleus that attracted much of the brilliant society of the time, including the two personages who had honoured me with a visit, and also two others, with one of whom I became slightly acquainted, and with the other I was upon terms of some intimacy. The first of these two was Benjamin Disraeli, the other Sir Edward Lytton Bulwer.

I met the former upon two occasions, both at a comparatively recent date. The first was at a dinner party given by Lord Henry Lennox. He sat next but one to me at the dinner table, but I had no conversation with him, and indeed he was very silent. Of course I was interested in observing him, and pleased with the opportunity which I was afforded of being introduced to him. I met him once afterwards at a garden party of the Prince of Wales at Chiswick. He was with Lady Beaconsfield; but although he spoke to me I doubt very much whether he knew who I was. He left to join some one, and not returning I saw Lady Beaconsfield to her carriage. I suppose that the sympathy exhibited by all classes and of every shade of politics during the illness that terminated in his death has never been surpassed.

The étiquette existing amongst medical men was curiously illustrated upon this occasion; but I confess that whilst I should be very loth to blame an adherence to rules that have been created both for the honour of the profession and the interest of the public, it is difficult not to feel that there are contingencies which would justify a deviation from them. I have reason to think that Dr. Quain entertained but little hope of his recovery from the first, and in this instance it cannot be said that the etiquette of the medical profession in any way interfered with the most skilful treatment of so illustrious a patient.[1]

I was well acquainted with the brother of Lord Beaconsfield from a very early period. He was a member of the Clarence Club. I also used to meet Montagu Corry, who not unfrequently joined the little corner that I have described at Paddy Green's; and although I knew so little of his lordship personally, I fancied that I could gather from the terms with which he was spoken of by others the clue to that affection he had the reputation of creating in the minds of all who had the pleasure of his intimate acquaintance.

---

[1] It is well known that a question arose about meeting Lord Beaconsfield's regular medical attendant, who professed homœopathy. No one has more rigidly maintained the honour of the profession than Dr. Quain, whom I am proud to call my friend; and the course of conduct he pursued was universally approved.

CHAPTER XXV.

LORD LYTTON.

WHEN Lord Lytton was Secretary of State for the
Colonies some papers were removed from the office
in which they had been deposited. This had
clearly been done surreptitiously, and it turned
out that the person doing it had been actuated by
some idea that he could obtain from their possession a personal benefit. Lord Lytton was greatly
annoyed. He thought that some reflection would
be cast upon him for want of sufficient care, and
he determined to prosecute the offender, who was
given into custody, and after which I was consulted by his solicitors upon the subject. Lord
Lytton requested that I would call upon him,
which I did one morning at No. 1 Park Lane,
where he then resided. I went at the time he appointed, and found him at breakfast.

I remember that he had several animals about
him, amongst others a parrot of which he appeared
to be very fond. He had always gone in for
artistic dress, and had shone in London another
star with Count D'Orsay. If I remember correctly

he was even then somewhat deaf. I thought that he attached to the affair far more consequence than it really deserved, as it was quite absurd to suppose that any one would dream of blaming him. However, the man was sent for trial at the Central Court and was made the subject of a State prosecution. Sir Fitzroy Kelly, then Attorney-General, conducted it with his accustomed solemnity. Serjeant Parry defended, and in a very able speech made the most of the importance that had been attached to a very trivial matter. Baron Martin summed up against the prisoner, as in law he was bound to do, but did it in a way to show that he should have been glad if the law had been otherwise, and the jury accommodated themselves to his views by acquitting him. From that time I used very frequently to meet Lord Lytton, and upon several occasions dined with him, both in Park Lane and afterwards in Grosvenor Square. He was certainly a man well worthy of record in the history of his generation.

As a statesman he is the property of history. He certainly possessed the merit of being most painstaking, and I should say almost too anxious. As an orator, his style was elaborate and his speeches most carefully prepared. The unfortunate infirmity of his deafness was a bar to his being an efficient debater. Of his literary works

I, in common with the rest of society, am able to form a judgment. They were very popular, and generally exhibited much care, research, and knowledge, and his novels certainly possessed what I may perhaps place too highly in the category of excellence, the power of amusing. It is difficult to imagine four writers of the period, all engaged in works of fiction, whose attributes were so entirely different as those of Thackeray, Dickens, Bulwer, and Disraeli, and the age is not to be despised in which they flourished. Of the two latter it must be remembered that other pursuits than that of literature principally occupied their minds.

It is no small compliment to Bulwer's dramatic compositions that several of his plays still hold possession of the stage. The principal parts, both male and female, have been played by the best of our actors and actresses, and still form the ambition of novices. ' The Lady of Lyons ' and 'Richelieu' are said to be stilted, but whenever they are performed by actors of intelligence they invariably command good audiences, and ' Money ' is always popular especially in the ' provinces.' The best performance that I ever witnessed of ' Richelieu ' was by Mr. Booth, the well-known American actor.

Lord Lytton consulted me upon another matter in which he had acted upon very bad advice, and which was a source of great annoyance to him, and

I am vain enough to believe that he placed considerable confidence in my opinion. I have upon several occasions remained with him after other guests had left. He was not a good conversationalist, as he was too didactic, and appeared rather to be giving a treatise than inviting a discussion, but what he said was very instructive as well as amusing. I noticed that he dwelt with great apparent pleasure upon the supernatural, and those who have read some of his works, 'Zanoni' for instance, and 'A Strange Story,' can scarcely doubt that he was strongly impregnated with a belief in it. It is very interesting to note the number of remarkable men who have exhibited similar impressions. They are rarely, if ever, boldly avowed, and are nearly always protested against ; but still the feeling creeps out, and it is also remarkable how willing the mass of people are to receive it with apparent concurrence.

I suppose that no one thinks ' Guy Mannering ' a supernatural novel, and yet the main interest of the story turns upon a horoscope cast by an Indian soldier, whilst Meg Merrilies, one of the most powerful of the author's characters, is clearly endowed with a spirit of prophecy, and we have never heard this most charming of works of fiction charged with improbability. I am convinced that Mr. Const, whom I have before mentioned, a lawyer

and a man of pleasure, one of all others whom I
should have thought least capable of fanciful ideas,
was fully possessed with the notion that he had
lived before. He kept a diary, recording events in
Latin, and once he lent me two or three pages
which detailed some incident in which I was interested, and there I found a scene in the description of which he stated that he recognised every
feature, and the actual spoken words, although he
never could have witnessed it during his present
life. When I was translating this aloud, he snatched
the diary from my hand.

I do not think it will be out of place whilst
upon this subject to relate a story told of Sir Astley
Cooper. I am not certain that it has not already
been in print, but I know that I have had frequent
conversations about it with his nephew.

There had been a murder, and Sir Astley was
upon the scene when a man suspected of it was
apprehended, and Sir Astley, being greatly interested, accompanied the officers with their prisoner to the gaol, and he and they and the
accused were all in a cell, locked in together,
when they noticed a little dog, which kept biting
at the skirt of the prisoner's coat. This led them
to examine the garment, and they found upon it
traces of blood, which ultimately led to the conviction of the man. When they looked round

the dog had disappeared, although the door had never been opened. How it had got there, or how it got away, nobody could tell. When Bransby Cooper spoke of this, he always said that of course his uncle had made a mistake, and was convinced of this himself; and Bransby used to add that, no doubt, if the matter had been investigated, it would have been shown that there was a mode of accounting for it from natural causes. But I believe that neither Sir Astley nor his nephew in their own hearts discarded entirely the supernatural.

In relating these anecdotes I am only recording how men of great intellect may be affected by such circumstances. I thought at one time that the last incident applied to the case of Patch, which I have told in a former chapter; but although it may do so I am unable to substantiate it, and must leave it therefore upon no more solid foundation than my memory of its relation to myself as having occurred during some portion of Sir Astley Cooper's early career.

Lord Lytton was extremely interested in criminal investigations, and I could always obtain his attention when I related any of those in which I had myself been engaged, and in novels that he had written previous to my acquaintance with him he had used the records of crime in their construc-

tion.   A leading idea in 'Pelham,' although the
details were dissimilar, was suggested by the case
of Thurtell, of which I have already given some
particulars; and there was a trial that took place
at the early part of the present century.   The
history of a person named Wainwright had furnished incidents very similar to those related in
the novel of 'Lucretia.'   In that case the man was
convicted of forgery and transported, but no doubt
whatever existed that he had also been a practised
poisoner.[1] I have always thought that the prologue
to this work was one of the most powerful pieces
of writing that ever came from Lord Lytton's pen.
He told me himself that the character of the
banker in 'The Disowned' was suggested by
Fauntleroy, and those who remember the history
of this man are aware that he was a voluptuary
as well as a forger.   Lord Lytton describes him
also as a craven; and I was able to relate an
anecdote that showed that this appreciation of his
character was correct.

At the time of the committal of Fauntleroy my
father was a visiting justice at Coldbath Fields, to
which prison he was sent.   An old Bow Street
officer—or runner, as these officials used to be
designated—of the name of Vickery was the
governor.   A suspicion arose that some one in the

[1] Before his death he confessed to having done so.

gaol had been tampered with to enable the prisoner to effect his escape, and my father assisted in the investigation of the circumstances, and I learnt from him that it was clearly proved that a ladder of ropes and other conveniences for escape had by some agency been supplied to him ; but, as was supposed by those engaged in the inquiry, his courage failed him, and he did not make the attempt.

Although ' The Disowned ' is an excellent and interesting work of fiction, the author has, I cannot help thinking, been guilty of a slight slip in one of the episodes contained in the work. A very graphic and amusing sketch is given of the arrest of the banker. He is supposed, before the crash had taken place, or anything was known about its probability, to have gone disguised to the White Horse Cellar, to have asked for a letter directed in an assumed name, and on reading it pretend that he was suddenly called abroad, and ordered a post-chaise. A police officer—why or wherefore is not stated—is seated in the room, orders another post-chaise, follows the banker, and apprehends him at Dover, exhibiting an amount of sagacity that even in those days was more than remarkable. I ventured once to draw Lord Lytton's attention to the difficulty presented to my mind, but got no explanation, and he did not seem to me to be much pleased with the subject.

Once when I was enjoying a somewhat con-fidential talk with him at the commencement of our acquaintance, I related an episode in my own life in which he seemed to take a kindly and sym-pathetic interest, and he afterwards embodied it with little alteration in one of his novels called 'What will He do with It?'

Lord Lytton was very fond of whist, and he and I both belonged to the well-known Portland Club, in which were to be found many of the cele-brated players of the day. He never showed the slightest disposition of a gambler. He played the game well, and without excitement or temper, and apparently his whole attention was concen-trated upon it; but it was curious to see that at every interval that occurred in the rubbers he would rush off to a writing-table, and with equally concentrated attention proceed with some literary work until called again to take his place at the whist-table. There was a member of the club, a very harmless, inoffensive man, of the name of Townend, for whom Lord Lytton entertained a mortal antipathy, and would never play whilst that gentleman was in the room. He firmly believed that he brought him bad luck. I was witness to what must be termed an odd coincidence. One afternoon, when Lord Lytton was playing, and had enjoyed an uninterrupted run of luck, it suddenly turned, upon which he exclaimed, ' I am sure that Mr. Townend has come into the club.' Some three minutes after, just time enough to ascend the stairs, in walked this unlucky personage. Lord Lytton, as soon as the rubber was over, left the table and did not renew the play.

The last time I saw Lord Lytton was after I had ceased to be a member of the club, but was invited to dine there by a Mr. Dommett, a very old and valued friend of mine. It was shortly before Lord Lytton's death. He was about going into Devonshire, and invited me to visit him there. I cannot remember whether he had just undergone or was about to undergo an operation with a view to ameliorate his deafness. Unhappily there was such an operation performed, resulting in an abscess, which, suppurating internally, caused his death. This event, I am certain, created great commiseration in all the circles where his unaffected courtesy, as well as other qualities, rendere l him a most agreeable and valued companion.

Amongst those who were cotemporary with Lord Lytton as a statesman, orator, and author—I have been tempted to say as a novelist, although such a description might be protested against— was Thomas Babington Macaulay, historian and

I might say poet, as I have often thought the painting of his hero William, whilst as vivid and inspiring, is just as fanciful as that of Claverhouse by Sir Walter Scott. Still, whether true or not to history, how much of delight has been afforded to the age we live in by that and other of his works! I confess I groan over his merciless onslaught upon Scott's gallant Highlander.

It is not, however, to criticise his works that I recall his name, but to mention that a very pleasing incident in my own life was making his acquaintance and travelling for three days in his company. He was with Mr. Ellis, an eminent lawyer and a friend of mine. We passed through some of the cities of Belgium. Every one has heard of his marvellous memory and his inexhaustible fund of information; he delighted to impart it. There was no subject about which he talked that he was not eloquent and instructive upon, and I did not at all regret that during the time I was in his company I myself was constrained to preserve almost uninterrupted silence.

In recording my recollections of Lord Lytton, I have not been sorry to introduce my readers to the Portland Club. It comprised amongst its members many well-known personages, with some of whom I was upon terms of intimacy.

It was considered to be a play club, not

similar to Crockford's and Graham's, as the games allowed were confined to such only as combined skill with chance, and, as I have previously mentioned, many first-rate players belonged to it. There was a dinner in the evening, which brought people together, and at which much good fellowship prevailed. The play at times was high, but a moderate game could generally be obtained by those who desired it.

When first I entered the club my attention was attracted by an active, lithesome old man engaged in a game of billiards, which, considering his age, he was playing with wonderful power and skill. This was ' the Squire ' Osbaldestone. He had filled for half a century before I knew him no small space in the sporting world, and it was not difficult to discover in him the weakness that had wrecked a fine fortune. Although few surpassed him in his knowledge of horses, and no amateur in riding them, and although he was a first-rate pedestrian, cricketer, and shot, he overestimated his powers in playing, as it were, against the field, and laid the odds on himself instead of obtaining them. He bore his fate with apparent equanimity, and the lessons he had received did not seem to have in any respect lessened his opinion of himself.

A very constant player at afternoon whist was Lord Henry Bentinck. His name, as may be remembered, was introduced with those of George

Anson and George Payne upon the Lord de Ros trial, and by itself would have been sufficient guarantee that no hasty or unconsidered charge had been launched against that unfortunate nobleman.

I think that Lord Henry was a man of considerable intellect, but he was extremely reserved, and although I have met him at Lord Lytton's and elsewhere, he furnished but few opportunities for forming a judgment. He was a fine whist player, indifferent to the stakes he played, and a rigid adherent to the rules of the game, from which, as he understood them, nothing would induce him to deviate.

An excited adversary might display by a gesture what he had in his hand, but it was lost upon Lord Henry; and if cards were exposed under his very nose, his eyes might see them, but it altered not his play. I can remember well a member, who did not so much respect accuracy in play as he did the result of it, gnashing his teeth at what he deemed the idiotism and folly of his lordship. There are many alive who may guess to whom I allude; he himself is dead.

I was once walking home with Lord Henry from a dinner party at Cavendish Square. He told me that Lord de Ros had received frequent warnings, but seemed blind to all of them; and from my perusal of the trial, and what I heard from his lordship, and from his evident view upon the subject, I am convinced that Lord de Ros furnished an example of a mind in most respects sound and intelligent, but subject to this one uncontrollable impulse. Lord Henry considered that no one surpassed himself in skill in any game that he played, but he told me that although in the long run he had been a winner, it was to a very trifling amount—saying, I remember, that he should have made more as a journeyman glazier!

Frederick Clay, the recognised authority upon the game of whist, was a member, and played frequently. There was an amusing rivalry between him and Lord Henry; each of them declared that the other knew nothing about the game. Mr. Clay was a great proficient in all games of skill. He was champion billiard player amongst amateurs. His work upon whist was recognised as the great authority until 'Cavendish' rather supplemented it than wrote a new one. He might, however, be remembered for higher qualities than these exhibit. He was extremely well informed, capable of taking correct and forcible views upon most subjects. In the House of Commons, where he sat for the borough of Hull, he was much looked up to, and his house

in Bryanston Square was the scene of many pleasant gatherings.

One of the most amusing companions I ever
met with, whether in this club or out of it, was
John Bushe, not a young man when first I made
his acquaintance, but full of life and good spirits.
He was an Irishman, and the son of the well-
known Chief Justice of the Irish Court of Common
Pleas, a judge whose witty sayings somewhat
startled the decorum of the Bench, even in times
not famous for that characteristic. His son was
bright and amusing, and his little parties in the
Albany were always highly appreciated. No one,
probably, had seen more of life in all its phases.
In the early part of it he had been engaged in
one or two 'affairs of honour,' as they were
called ; there were few Irishmen who had not
been, but no one could be less prone to quarrel
than he was, or possess a more perfectly even
temper. He was a good player at most games,
and, as may be supposed, very popular in the
club.

There is still a figure that I recall, indeed it
would be very difficult to forget it—Dr. Jones,
father of 'Cavendish,' and himself as good a whist
player as his son the author of its rules, who also
belonged to the club.

I have frequently played a rubber with another member, whose name became famous during the Crimean War—General Windham. The gallantry universally exhibited during that memorable struggle has prevented individual traits from standing prominently forth upon many of the occasions on which they were exhibited; but Windham was fortunate in the particular event which has rendered his name celebrated, and even more fortunate in the eloquent and able pen that has connected it with the storming of the Redan. For this he is indebted to William Russell, of whom I believe I may say, without prejudice to others, that he created what has become an institution—the 'military correspondent' to a newspaper. His career and his example have been ably followed, and it would be difficult to exaggerate the qualities necessary for the performance of the duties involved. It requires not only literary attainment of no mean order, but he must be a man possessing military knowledge, unflinching courage, and great powers of endurance. It was in an ardent desire to fulfil his duties that my poor friend Boultby, as I have previously mentioned, became the victim of Chinese barbarity.

I knew Russell well in the early part of my career, and before he had made his name famous; and, although not thrown much into his society, we have met at the Garrick Club and elsewhere during the intervals of his freedom from work. He, like so many who bear honoured names, is an Irishman, and it was through some of my friends belonging to that country that I first made his acquaintance.

Kingston is an old friend of mine, and, apart from his professional merits, would, I am sure, enliven the dullest of campaigns. The reputation of Forbes and others cannot be enhanced by anything I say. I only regret that I do not possess the personal knowledge of them to enable me to add to the interest of these pages.

The Crimea—nearly thirty years have elapsed since the name became famous in English annals. The reality of the war was scarcely dreamt of by its authors, and I do not believe that any such terrible conflict was expected. I know that Lord Raglan, when he rearranged his insurances, stated with confidence that the expedition would be a merely military march.

I remember the event in connection with its social aspect, and even at this distance of time I can recall happy young faces that before the event I have seen at the Garrick Club and at Evans's, and with the owners of which I have often enjoyed myself, who soon after found their graves in a foreign land. The war made a sad clearance in many a place of amusement, but now that the

pangs first experienced have become deadened by
time, there is many a family reconciled to a loss
that has left a noble fame behind.

  One of the most amusing evenings that I ever
passed in my life was with one to whom before the
war I had bidden good-bye, and who, having been
upon nearly every battle-field through the campaign, and become the proud possessor of the
Victoria Cross, had escaped without a wound—
Colonel Goodlake. How he did escape is one of
those marvels difficult to be accounted for, as he
stood about six feet five in his boots, and presented a corresponding breadth of person. I dined
with him _tête-à-tête_ at the Tower on one night
shortly after his return, and listened with intense
interest to his simple but not less graphic details
of the different fights, and his affecting account
of deaths of lads whom we had both known. I
was filled with admiration for the courage and
endurance of our soldiers, officers and men, and
with a detestation and horror of what is called ' the
glory of war.'

  It is a general trait of great men in all professions that they rarely blazon their own exploits,
and this applies signally to those belonging to the
military profession. My old friend, Colonel Napier
Sturt, himself a Crimean officer, when on guard at
St. James's Palace, gave me frequent opportunities

of meeting his comrades at very agreeable dinner parties, and of listening to anecdotes, serious and gay, of the campaign.

Amongst the latter I was much amused by one told me, that an attack made upon a hamper of good things which had suddenly invaded their quarters invalided more men in the regiment than the fire of the enemy.

At one of these entertainments I met Mr. Greville, whose 'Memoirs' have caused so great a stir. He talked agreeably, but said very little, and seemed somewhat bored. I have read with great interest his recollections, and certainly his life ought to have furnished him with incessant enjoyment, mixing as he did with all that was famous and intellectual in society; but if the entry he made in his diary when he attained his fortieth birthday was a true index of his feelings, the reader would be apt to exclaim, 'All is indeed vanity!'[1]

[1] See Appendix.

END OF THE FIRST VOLUME.

S. & H.

Spottiswoode & Co., Printers, New-street Square, London.

VOL. I.   Y

CPSIA information can be obtained at www.ICGtesting.com
Printed in the USA
BVOW04s1005190514

353940BV00021B/1045/P

9 781162 966700